To: Katherine,

Enjoy!

Nancy

the uncomplicated gourmet
easy, elegant and economical recipes

Nancy Stern, CCP
certified culinary professional

the uncomplicated gourmet

Published by Author, Inc.
http://cookspalate.com

Libarary of Congress Control Number: 2009903734
ISBN: 9780981940458

Printed in the United States of America.
First printing: 2009

Editorial and production: Christy Anne Kuzmuk
Art design: Nancy Stern
Cover Design: Suzanne Brown- DesignOnline

Photography:
Memories TTL, LLC, Wing Wong
Kate's Casual Portraits, Kate Jackson
Nancy Stern

Table of Contents

Acknowledgements

FOR:

My husband, Donald, for 50 years of love and support
My children, Cliff and Wendy, for their appreciation
My grandchildren, Alec, Remy and Jaden, for their enthusiasm
My friends (all of you) for your consumption
My students for your faith in me
and to my assistant, Christy, for keeping me on track.

It is for all of you that I have finally put this collection together.

Enjoy them, use them frequently and don't be afraid to make mistakes...
some of my best recipes happened that way.
After forty years of cooking, eating, teaching and sharing food...
the thing that stands out most, is to not take it all too seriously.

After all, it is still just one meal out of the thousands you will consume in a lifetime.
The Uncomplicated Gourmet is not just a cookbook, it is a way of life.

Introduction

My love of cooking began when I was three or four in the kitchen of a small hotel in the Adirondacks called the Chalet Swiss. The chef/owner, William Muller, and his wife, Hilda, became the driving force of my passion for food. On the hot summer days before air-conditioning, I would sit in the kitchen and inhale the pungent aromas of that wonderful space. Sitting on a stool and shelling peas and stringing beans, I would listen to the sounds of the sizzling in the skillets. It was music to my young ears.

Since, as a child, I had the good fortune to travel with my family, I saw how food was presented in the elegant hotels we visited. Over the next 15 years, I would experiment in my mothers kitchen with all kinds of food combinations. I knew instinctively that it was not always how the food tasted that was key to its success. Making a dish attractive would entice people to sample what was presented, even if it was not their favorite food.

In 1967, I was the mother of a three year old son and a one year old daughter. I was living in suburbia with my husband in a split level home that I was thrilled to own. Days were filled with activities centered on the children. Somehow, I was always cooking and entertaining at home. Slowly, but surely, friends asked me if I would help them out with parties. I started cooking for friends. Then I started cooking for friends of friends and that became "catering." After the children went to bed at night, I would cook until 2-3 a.m. The only thing my husband put his two cents in on was to plead with me not to fry egg rolls in the middle of the night because the aroma would make him insanely hungry and he would want another meal.

By 1969, I was cooking more and more. At the same time, my friend, Lyn Valger, and I opened a baby gift business called "Creative Gifts." With our husbands, we would share grownup dinners three to four nights a week. Lyn, who was an excellent baker, would make a great dessert. We would open a bottle of wine and talk about the daily events in our lives. On the weekend, we would venture to Chinatown in New York City with friends to have Chinese Banquets. Our lives were truly about the children, work and food.

I learned many great cooking skills in the kitchens of the restaurants that we frequented. All I had to do was ask and I would be next to the chef learning the tricks of the trade without working the line in the restaurant. This applied to all kinds of cuisine. If you cook, you share a passion with all that find it "not too hot to stay in the kitchen."

In the fall of 1969, a friend called and said they were liking for a cooking teacher for the adult education department of Glen Rock, New Jersey. Would I be interested? I didn't know if I could do it, so I called a group of friends to come for a trial lesson. They were seated in my diningroom. I would race around the corner to the kitchen and prepare something and then back around the corner to the diningroom to explain it to them. And so it went for a whole afternoon. My original kitchen was eleven by twelve feet with three doors and a large dog crate in the center that became an island. After that lesson, everyone agreed that it was truly their impression of gourmet food and was very uncomplicated. When I named the first class it became "The Uncomplicated Gourmet" and has become a registered trademark in the years that followed, but more about that later.

I had been teaching for years before my mentor, Willie, allowed me to touch the pots in his kitchen. After the season, before he returned to New York City and his real job of head chef at the Louis Sherry Restaurant in the old Metropolitan Opera House, we would cook together, eat and play Swiss card games. Next door to the Chalet was and still is the best smoke house in the East, Oscars Smokehouse. You could become "heady" from the smell in the air all day and night....envision living in a bacon factory, for that is what it is. Today the Chalet is gone but we still make our pilgrimage to Oscars several times a year.

In 1974, I was asked to do an ongoing series of classes at the Abraham and Straus department store in Paramus, N.J. I became a very close friend to the events director, Arlyn Blake. She hired me to do three two-hour classes each week, as well as, demonstrating small appliances and judging food contests.

In 1978, Arlyn was asked to interview for a spokesperson position and since she had just returned to college to finish her degree, she recommended me to the public relations firm. I interviewed several times with them and the client, Proctor and Gamble, before landing the role of spokesperson for Pringles Potato Chips. I went on the road to do radio, TV and newspaper interviews. My job was to tell the world that Pringles had "no artificial ingredients or preservatives." It was a 45 city tour that lasted one year and was probably one of the most interesting experiences of my teaching career.

In addition to seeing the United States on someone else's dollar, I earned enough to build my teaching kitchen in our home. That little kitchen grew to 22 X 24 feet with an island, twelve feet by five feet, that could seat a class of ten. Now, thirty years later, it looks as though it was done yesterday. I was so ahead of my time! My livingroom, diningroom and kitchen are one big space...enough to seat three tables of ten for a sit down meal. " If you cook, they will come." Over the years we have hosted everyone's bridal shower, baby shower, engagement party, as well as, Thanksgivings, Passover Seders and reunions in this wonderful space.

In the year that followed I went on the road teaching the "hors d'oeuvre dinner party" featuring Pringles Potato Chips, I was aware that I had a really good hook in "The Uncomplicated Gourmet" title. Before leaving for my very first city, I trade marked the name and it has been my registered mark ever since. I had used the whisk as my logo when I first started teaching and it, too, was trade marked for teaching.

In order to keep an active income, I was also developing housewares products, doing recipe development for manufactures, and doing guest lecturing at various cooking schools.

In 1978, I joined the International Association of Cooking Teachers (later changed to International Association of Culinary Professionals.) I became a certified culinary professional by sitting for the six hour exam. I have kept up my education by attending seminars and conventions for this past thirty years.

During the expansion of the house, I became very involved in the construction and learned on a daily basis more about what was being done. My art background led me to designing kitchens and seeing how the practical interacted with the beautiful. By 1985, when standing on my feet cooking for fifteen hours a day became physically impossible, I started looking around for another career. I had always designed kitchens for friends and then when I would visit the finished projects be astounded at what what I saw. It had been done so poorly. I answered an ad for a showroom that needed a designer and as Groucho Marx said, "Any club that would take him as a member, he wouldn't care to belong to." I should have never gone to work for this company!

The first day I was taken out to learn to measure and the next week I saw 20 clients and worked every night producing free estimates. By the end of the first month, I knew that I had more knowledge of what I was doing than they did. I stayed for six months to recover my good name and see the customers through their law suits. It dawned on me that my ethics and those of others did not mesh and went on my own. Since I was virtually invisible, I began teaching a class called "So You Want a New Kitchen" in all the locations that I formerly taught cooking. To this day, I see people who say, "I took your class two years ago and I am now ready to do my kitchen."

In 1996, I opened Elements for Kitchen, Bath and Home, inc. in Riverdale, New Jersey. I am in the Bograd's Furniture Center just of exit 53 of Route 287. The showroom has always been on the cutting edge of design and function. Beautiful kitchens are easy but ones that work are not. Because I am one of two certified culinary professionals in America who do kitchens full time, I serve people who do not just want the kitchen to look exquisite but to also perform well. Because I both cook and teach, I have never been far from the culinary world. I have continued to teach cooking both in the showroom and at other locations for all these years. Now, after these forty years in the kitchen, I am spending time at the computer sharing the recipes that have exemplified the name - The Uncomplicated Gourmet.

To see some examples of my work visit my portfolio on my web site:
www.elementsforkitchens.com

P.S. Be sure to read the <u>entire</u> recipe before beginning to cook. Take out and measure your ingredients. Now, there will be no surprises and the dishes will be easy to prepare.

the uncomplicated gourmet

Appetizers

Make an entire dinner party of a balanced assortment of hor d'oeuvres.
No one will miss a sit down meal.

Eggplant Oriental, p.19

Arlene's Gorgonzola-Pistachio Torte, p. 12

Eggplant Spread, p. 20

Appetizer Flan in an Eggshell, p. 11

Pauline's Chopped Chicken Liver, p. 30

Appetizer Flan in an Eggshell

Recipe Notes
I have used crabmeat sauteed in butter and brandy as a filling under the custard.
There are as many variations as your mind can conger.

8	brown eggs
1	cup heavy cream
3/4	teaspoon salt
1	teaspoon white pepper, freshly ground
1/4	cup chives, chopped
6	ounces smoked salmon
8	chive stalks with blossom if available or just stalks

Instructions
Preheat oven to 350°.

Cut the top off each egg. There is a special cutter used for soft boiled eggs that is great for this or just use a scissor.

Put four of the eggs in a bowl and beat with the cup of cream. Season with salt and pepper and set aside. Reserve the rest of the eggs for another purpose. Rinse the shells with water and invert to dry.

Mince half the salmon and mix with the chopped chives.

Place the eight egg shells, cut side up in a cardboard egg carton. Do not use plastic. If you have mini muffins tins, they work as well.

Put a tablespoon of minced salmon in the bottom of each egg shell.

Put the cream mixture in a measuring cup with a lip and fill each egg 3/4 full. Put the carton in a roasting pan and pour in about one inch of water.

Cover with foil and bake 30 minutes. Remove eggs from carton and place in individual egg cups or demi tasse cups.

Cut remaining salmon in strips and place on top of each egg.
Put a chive stalk or whole chive plume in each egg for presentation. Serve with a demi tasse spoon on each plate.

Serves: 8.

Arlene's Gorgonzola-Pistachio Torte

<u>Recipe Notes</u>
This was Arlene Ward's recipe that I have enjoyed making for many years. I think you will enjoy it, too.
Special cheese torte for the buffet table and large parties.

32	ounces cream cheese
16	ounces unsalted butter
8	ounces brie
8	ounces gorgonzola cheese
1	bunch parsley, chopped
1/2	cup pistachio nuts, chopped
1	bunch scallions, chopped

Instructions

Bring cream cheese, butter and gorgonzola to room temperature. Trim rind off of brie and gorgonzola. Mix parsley and scallions with pistachios.

Line an eight inch springform pan with plastic wrap; set aside.

Beat ½ the cream cheese with butter and brie. Line the bottom of pan with cheese mixture. Top cheese with ½ parsley nut mixture. Beat remaining cheese with gorgonzola. Spread in pan and top with remaining nut mixture. Fold in plastic wrap to cover. Chill overnight. Unmold and press additional chopped parsley around sides.

Serves: 8.

Candied Bacon

Recipe Notes
This wonderful crisp spicy sweet treat is good as an appetizer but goes perfectly on the breakfast or brunch menu as well.

1	pound thick bacon
1/2	cup brown sugar
1	teaspoon cayenne pepper
1/2	teaspoon black pepper

Instructions

Preheat the oven to 425°.

Take 2 rimmed cookie sheets and put a rack on each.

Mix the seasonings with the brown sugar and put on a flat dish. Press each side of the bacon slices in the mixture and place on racks on cookie sheets. (You will need both sheets)

Bake about 10 minutes and drain off fat.

Bake until crispy about 10 minutes more.

Drain fat as it accumulates so that there is no smoke.

Lift bacon from rack and blot off any extra fat. Keep warm or let come to room temperature.

Serves: 12.

Carmelized Onions

Recipe Notes
You can use any type of onions for this recipe, including red onions.

Spread crostini with goat cheese and top with onions as a tasty hors d'oeuvre.

You can mix 1/2 cup of these onions with 1 pt. sour cream and 4 oz. cream cheese to make a dip for veggies or chips.

3	pounds any onions, peeled (Red ones are very pretty)
1/4	cup canola oil
1/3	cup cider vinegar
1	teaspoon coriander ground
1/2	teaspoon allspice ground
1	cup brown sugar
1/2	cup maple syrup

Instructions

Thinly slice and place in a 2 quart pot with the oil. Cook until the onions are soft. Add the remaining ingredients and bring to a boil. Reduce the heat and simmer for about 1½ hours until thickened and caramelized. Could take longer depending on the moisture in the onions.

Serves: 8.

Caviar Pie

<u>Recipe Notes</u>
This is a pretty presentation of egg salad with a twist.
Be sure to cut out a wedge or no one will touch it.
Pretty food is nice but it has to look approachable.
To hard boil an egg: place in a 2 quart pot and cover with cold water.
Bring the water to a boil and cover the pot. Turn off the heat. Let sit 10 minutes and then pour off water and run under cold water to cool the eggs.

5	large eggs, hard boiled
2	teaspoons onions, grated
2	teaspoons mayonnaise
1	jar Caviar
3	ounces cream cheese
3/4	cup sour cream
1/2	cup parsley, minced
1	loaf party pumpernickel bread
1	whole pimiento, sliced lengthwise

Instructions

Red salmon caviar is the best to use for this...do not waste the expensive stuff!

Chop the eggs coarsely and add the onion. Stir in enough mayo to make a stiff egg salad. Don't make it too wet.

Spread on the bottom of a 6 inch pie plate or decorative candy plate or soup bowl. Spread the caviar carefully over the eggs to 1/2" from the edge.

Beat the cream cheese and the sour cream until smooth. Delicately frost the pie covering caviar completely. Use the parsley to make an attractive rim around the edge of the plate.

For Christmas use the pimentos to make bows.

Cover loosely with plastic wrap and chill several hours. Serve with the pumpernickel.

Serves: 8.

Chinese Sausage Sliders

Recipe Notes
An Asian grocery is the best place to find the sausages...if you can't find them....change the whole recipe to Italian and use spicy marinara and cooked spicy chicken sausages cut into small dice. Have fun making your own versions of this tasty treat.

1	can small biscuits (10-12 biscuits)
1	pound Chinese Sausages, narrow ones with sugar in meat mixture
8	ounces Hoisin Sauce
1	tablespoon sesame oil
3	tablespoons soy sauce
1	teaspoon hot (spicy) chili oil
4	whole scallions, chopped

Instructions

Bake biscuits according to directions on the can. Brush the tops with extra sesame oil before baking.

Dice the sausages in quarter inch pieces.

Combine hoisin sauce, soy sauce, sesame oil, and chili oil in a quart pot. Heat until bubbling and add the sausages. Cook for 10-15 minutes. Stir in scallions.

Split the biscuits horizontally and put in 2 Tbsp. of filling. Replace the tops and serve.

Makes 10-12.

Chinese Scallion Pancakes

<u>Recipe Notes</u>
These are addictive so make plenty. I freeze them cooked and reheat in 350° oven for 10-15 minutes.

2	cups flour
1	teaspoon salt
1	cup water, boiling
1	tablespoon sesame oil
1	cup peanut oil
1/2	cup scallions, chopped

Instructions

Put flour in the bowl of the food processor with salt. Pulse on/off. Turn on machine and pour boiling water down the feed tube... a bowl of dough will form immediately. Let spin a few seconds to knead. (The Chinese do this by hand with chop sticks...I found that this way was easier.)

Place dough in a bowl and cover with a damp cloth. Set aside 30 minutes.

On a well floured cloth or board roll out dough 1/4" thick and approximately 10" x 15". Brush slightly with peanut oil and scatter chopped scallions evenly on top. Roll the dough up like a jelly roll. Cut into 6 thick slices. Flatten each piece slightly and roll on well-floured cloth or board to approx. 6" circles. Cover finished pancakes with a cloth as you work.

Heat peanut oil 1/4" deep in a small skillet. When oil is hot reduce heat to medium. Cookone side of each side until golden brown turn and cook other side. Repeat with all pancakes. Cut into 4 wedges each and serve with:

Chinese Soy Sauce Dipping Sauce
1/3 cup seasoned rice wine vinegar
2 tablespoon water
1/3 cup lite soy sauce
1 teaspoon sesame oil or spicy sesame oil
3 whole scallions, minced

Shake all the ingredients in a small jar and put in a dish to spoon onto the pancakes before eating.

Serves: 8.

Corn Fritters

Recipe Notes
These can be made in advance and put on a cookie sheet in the freezer (uncovered) until solid. When frozen bag and store. Reheat, from frozen, as many as needed in 425 ° oven for 10 minutes.

Do not touch your face while handling the jalapenos and be sure to wash your hands when you are done.

1	cup onion, minced
2	tablespoons olive oil
1	jalapeno pepper, minced
1	cup pancake or biscuit mix
1	egg, separated
3/4	cup milk
1 1/2	teaspoons canola oil
1	cup corn, canned

Instructions

You will need additional canola oil for frying.

Saute onion and jalapeno (without the seeds) in 2T. olive oil until wilted but not brown. Set aside to cool.

Measure the pancake or biscuit mix into a medium bowl.

In a large bowl, beat the egg yolk, milk, and canola oil together. Gradually add pancake mix. Stir to just moisten.

Beat the egg white until stiff; fold it into the batter. Drain the corn and gently fold into the batter. Fold in the jalapeno – onion mixture.

Heat oil in deep fryer or deep skillet to 365°. Drop batter by tablespoonfuls into hot oil, cooking just a few at a time. Do not overcrowd the pan. Fry until fritters are puffed and browned, turning once. Drain fritters on paper towel and salt immediately. Serve hot.

Serves: 10.

Eggplant Oriental

Recipe Notes
This is the recipe of my mentor, Willie Muller. It is a wonderful appetizer or first course at the table or on greens as a salad course.

2	tablespoons olive oil
4	cloves garlic, minced
1	large eggplant, thinly sliced
3	large onions, thinly sliced
5	tomatoes, sliced
1	red bell pepper, cut into strips
1	green bell pepper, cut into strips
1/2	cup vegetable oil
1/3	cup red wine vinegar
1	cup ketchup
3/4	cup water
1	bay leaf
1/2	teaspoon dried oregano
1/2	teaspoon dried basil

Instructions

Preheat the oven to 350°.

Spread the oil over the bottom of a large metal or glass roasting pan and scatter the garlic over the oil. Alternate the slices of eggplant, onion and tomato in overlapping rows. Place the wedges of the peppers between the rows and then mix the rest of the ingredients to make a dressing. Pour the dressing mixture evenly over all. Cover tightly with a piece of foil and bake 45-50 minutes. Cool and then chill in the pan.

Serve chilled on individual small plates.

Serves: 10.

Eggplant Spread

Recipe Notes
This is another one of grandma Sylvia's tried and true.

1	medium eggplant
2	green peppers
2	small raw onions, minced
2	large garlic cloves, minced
1/2	cup olive oil
1/4	cup white wine vinegar
1/4	teaspoon salt
1	freshly ground black pepper to taste

Instructions

Broil the eggplant and peppers about 4" from the flame, turning a quarter turn as each side browns. Put into a covered pot and wait 15 minutes. Carefully peel off outer skins and discard them. Discard the seeds and stem end. Chop together the eggplant and peppers with a knife or hand held chopper. Add onions and garlic. Mix together oil, vinegar, salt and freshly ground pepper (to taste) and stir into the eggplant. Marinate at least overnight.

Letting marinate for several days is better.

Serves: 8.

Gravad Lax

<u>Recipe Notes</u>
When you buy the fish, buy a matching top and bottom piece of equal size.

2	pounds Salmon Fillet
6	tablespoons kosher salt
3	tablespoons sugar
1	tablespoon freshly ground black pepper
1	large bunch of dill

Instructions

Make sure that there are no small bones in the fish. Wipe with a damp cloth.

Mix the salt, sugar and pepper together.

Use a glass dish the size of the fillet and place a third of dill in the bottom.

Rub ½ the salt mix on the first fillet and place skin side down on dill. Place another third of the dill on the fillet and rub other piece of fish with the rest of the salt mix.

Place 2nd fillet over the dill with skin side up.

Place remaining dill on top. Cover with a piece of plastic wrap. Put a small board on top and weight down with a brick or cans. Leave in the fridge for 12 hours. Remove weights and wrap. Turn over the fillets so bottom one is on top skin side up.

Recover and weight. Leave a minimum of 12 hours more. You can go up to 18 hours before rinsing, drying, and serving. Place fillet on cutting board and slice witha long slicing knife into thin pieces. Serve on party pumpernickel with mustard sauce.

Mustard sauce: Whisk together 3 Tbsp. Dijon mustard,3 Tbsp. sugar, 1 Tbsp. white wine vinegar, 3 Tbsp. canola oil, ¼ tsp. salt, few grinds pepper, 1 Tbsp. finely chopped fresh dill. Spoon on top of salmon.

Serves: 12.

Homemade Boursin Cheese

Recipe Notes
This is so easy and available with ingredients you have on hand. Fill celery sticks, endive leaves or pepper strips for a light snack.

8	ounces cream cheese, softened
3	tablespoons unsalted butter
1	tablespoon fresh parsley, minced
2	cloves garlic, minced
1/2	teaspoon dried oregano
1/8	teaspoon Tabasco sauce
1/2	tablespoon fresh chives, minced

Instructions

Stir all the ingredients together and then chill for about 2 hours, until it can hold its shape. Stuff into a mold or spread on crackers.

Serves: 6.

Homemade Guacamole

Recipe Notes
You can vary this every time with the addition of 1/2 cup chunkly salsa. There are lots of flavors of salsa available so experiment.

If your crowd likes cilantro, add a tablespoon of fresh minced....ask first , since there those to whom this tastes very nasty!

1	large avocado
1	small onion, chopped
2	cloves garlic, minced
2	tablespoons lemon juice
1	teaspoon Worcestershire sauce
1/2	teaspoon salt
1/8	teaspoon cayenne pepper
1/2	cup sour cream

Instructions

Put avocado, onion, and garlic in the bowl of the food processor. Add the rest of the ingredients and blend until smooth. Serve as a dip with corn chips or as a filling for omelettes.

Serves: 4.

Layered Taco Platter

Recipe Notes
Oldie but a goodie that everyone loves! Also called seven layer dip.

1	12 oz. can refried beans
1	tablespoon sour cream
1	package guacamole, prepared
1/2	cup sour cream
2	cups shredded lettuce
1	bunch scallions, chopped
1	cup black olives, pitted & sliced
1	can green chilies, chopped
1	cup shredded cheddar cheese
8	ounces taco sauce

Instructions

Mix the can of refried beans with 1 tbsp. of sour cream in food processor and blend until smooth.

Spread the bean dip on a large platter leaving a 2 inch wide border around edge.

Center the guacamole on the dip, spread to the edge of bean dip, spread sour cream on top leaving a border of guacamole.

Arrange the shreaded lettuce around the edge of the platter.

Scatter the top with scallions, chilies, and black olives. Top with shredded cheddar cheese and drizzle taco sauce over all. Serve with tortilla chips or Scoops.

Serves: 8.

Mark's Spicy Wing Dip

Recipe Notes

You never know where a recipe will come from.
This is from my UPS man, Mark Hettrich. It is his'"go to" dish for parties.
Obviously a "Super Bowl Favorite!."

If you have leftover cooked chicken, shred it well and use for this great dip.

2	20 ounce cans chicken (or buy a roasted chicken and shred all the meat)
3/4	cup hot sauce
1	cup Ranch Dressing
2	cups sharp cheddar cheese, shredded
16	ounces cream cheese

Instructions

Break up or shred the chicken thoroughly. Heat the chicken and the hot sauce in a large pot. When bubbling, add the rest of the ingredients and heat thoroughly.

Pour into a vessel that you can keep warm.

Serve with chips or veggies.

Serves: 24.

Miracle Mushrooms

Recipe Notes
The best for so little effort.
Baby Bella mushrooms are very tasty, too.

1	pound white mushrooms, sliced
1	cup heavy cream
1/2	teaspoon freshly ground black pepper
1/2	teaspoon salt
1	Juice of half a lemon

Instructions

Place the mushrooms in a large skillet.

Pour on the cream, add salt and pepper. Add the lemon juice. Let them cook over low heat for about 20 minutes, stirring occasionally. They will thicken into a delectable spread.

Place in a ramekin or serving bowl and surround with toasts or crackers.

Serves: 8.

Miserly Meatballs

Recipe Notes

*This is that old recipe that won't go away. Everyone loves these.
You can change the jelly, change the chili sauce to BBQ sauce
or add mustard and make it your own.*

If you use a baby ice cream scoop, you will make these all the same size. Ice cream scoops are the perfect tools for measuring servings of everything from cookie dough to mashed potatoes.

1 1/2	pounds beef chuck, ground
8	ounces grape jelly
12	ounces chili sauce

Instructions

Combine the jelly and chili sauce in a three quart pot. Make small meat balls of the beef and drop directly into the sauce. Let cook for about 50-60 minutes. Cool and chill overnight. Remove the congealed fat from the top and reheat to serve.

Substitute the grape jelly with apricot jam and use soy sauce and sesame oil to make this a Chinese version.

Serves: 12.

Mock Puff Pastry

Recipe Notes
For fillings: cheese with anything, shrimp with mayonnaise, mushrooms with herbs and butter etc....

You could wrap yesterday's leftovers in this dough and serve it as hors d'ouvres.

With a sweet filling , like pie filling, these can be nice small pastry bites.

1/2	pound unsalted butter
2	cups all-purpose flour
1/2	cup sour cream

Instructions

Cut together butter and flour with pastry blender and then stir in the sour cream until completely blended. Shape into 4 equal disks and wrap in waxed paper. Refrigerate for at least 6 hours.

Remove one disk from the refrigerator.

Prepare a well floured pastry cloth and rolling pin sleeve.* Roll the dough about 1/8" thick. Fill and seal the hors d'ouvres and brush the tops with beaten egg yolk or whole egg.

*You can also roll the pastry between two sheet of waxed paper.

Bake in 425° oven for about 10-12 minutes until nicely browned.

Serves: 10.

Nachos

<u>Recipe Notes</u>
Really quick if you use a microwave! (1 1/2 minutes on 80 % power)

Somehow, my to go to food when I am alone is always cheese...this just makes plain cheese better... and a lot more caloric... I try not to be alone too often!

1	package nacho chips
1/2	pound sharp cheddar cheese, shredded
1	jar Medium Salsa

Instructions

Heat oven to 375°.

Cover a cookie sheet with parchment paper or use a silpat. Place chips in a single layer and top with cheese, sauce and anything else you like. Bake until cheese melts, 5-8 minutes.

Serves: 8.

Pauline's Chopped Liver

Recipe Notes
I usually make this for the holidays...a few other times a year would be terrific, too.

Party pumpernickle, toasts and matzohs are good bases.

1	cup canola oil
3	large onions, finely chopped
1	pound chicken liver
2	eggs, hard boiled
2	teaspoons salt

Instructions

Saute the chopped onions in the oil until browned but not burned. Remove from heat when brown because they will continue to cook from the heat of the oil. Reserve 1/8 cup of onions and oil, then store the rest in fridge for another time.....they really stay a long time.

Wash and drain the livers removing any attached fat or sinews.

Boil the livers in water to cover for about 10 minutes until they are not pink on the inside side. Drain well.

Chop together the livers, eggs and the 1/8 cup of the reserved onions and oil. You may need to add more oil, a tablespoon at a time, to make it quite moist. Use any method that is easiest for you to chop: ie. knives, forks, chopper but do not use a blender.

I use the food processor. Cut the eggs in quarters and put in the bowl of processor. Add the livers to the bowl with 2 heaping tablespoons of onions and oil. Add salt. Pulse on and off until chopped but not creamy. Taste for the salt. Add more if needed. It will take a lot of salt.

Serves: 8.

Pauline's Potato Latkes

Recipe Notes

These are the best potato pancakes ever! They are easier than most and can be had anytime of the year as an appetizer. Top with homemade apple sauce, smoked salmon, sour cream or whatever you like.

You can make these larger by using a serving spoon. Cook them longer and serve as a side dish to meat or poultry. After draining, put on a foil lined cookie sheet. Place open in the freezer and when frozen, bag and use as needed by heating for 10 minutes in 400 ° oven.

2	large Idaho potatoes
1	large yellow onion
2	whole eggs
1	egg yolk
1/4	teaspoon baking powder
1	tablespoon salt
1/2	cup Matzoh meal or cracker crumbs
1/2	cup canola oil for frying

Instructions

Peel the potatoes and cut into one inch pieces. Place in cold water. Cut onion into one inch pieces. Drain and dry the potatoes. Place the two eggs and extra yolk in the blender. Pulse to mix. Add the onion and pulse until finely chopped. Add the potatoes, salt and baking powder and pulse until just chopped and no large pieces remain. Pour into a large bowl, and stir in the 1/2 cup of matzoh meal to absorb the liguid. Add enough so that it is not soupy.

Heat 1/8 inch canola oil in a large skillet over medium heat.You may need to add more oil when frying all the latkes. When hot, drop in the batter by tablespoonfuls and brown on one side then turn and brown on the other. Cook about six at a time. Remove to a paper towel to drain. Repeat until batter is finished.

Serves: 8.

Shrimp Cocktail

Recipe Notes
Buy cooked shrimp if you must... but it is easy to cook your own.

For a buffet: you can lip the shrimp on the side of a bowl filled with ice and place the cocktail sauce in the center.

1 1/2	pounds Shrimp (cleaned), 16-20 count
1	lemon, cut in half
4	peppercorns
2	teaspoons salt
1	cup ketchup
2	tablespoons hot horseradish
1	Juice of one lemon
1/2	teaspoon Worcestershire sauce
2	dashes Tabasco sauce (more if you like)

Instructions

Bring 2 quarts of water to a boil with lemon, peppercorns and salt.

Drop in shrimp and stir. Cook only until they have turned pink. About two- three minutes. Remove with slotted spoon to bowl of ice and chill throughly.

In a small bowl, combine: the ketchup, horseradish, lemon, worcestershire and add Tabasco to taste.

Place sauce in individual small dishes and surround with equal amounts of shrimp.

Serves: 6.

Spanish Spiced Nuts

Recipe Notes
I serve these nuts as an hors d'oeuvre. People can't get enough of them. I also found apricot kernels and made them the same way.

Any nut or mixture of nuts will be delicious with this topping.

1	large egg white
2	cups raw almonds
2	teaspoons salt
1	tablespoon cumin
1	tablespoon smoked paprika
1/2	teaspoon cayenne pepper
1/2	cup brown sugar

Instructions

Preheat oven to 350°.

Lightly beat the egg white in a medium sized bowl. Stir the almonds with the egg white until completely coated.

In another bowl, mix the spices together with the brown sugar. Mix in the brown sugar- spice mixture with the almonds.

Turn onto a parchment lined, rimmed cookie sheet and spread one layer thick. Bake for 30 minutes until the sugar is bubbling and the almonds are browned. Remove the parchment and place on a rack to cool.

When they are cool, the almonds will be crisp and brittle-like. Break into individual nut or small clusters.

Serves: 8.

Tuna Puffs

Recipe Notes
You could use canned salmon if you like. Add other spices like cayenne or cilantro for different undertones of flavor.

1	8 oz. can tuna in water, drained
2	egg whites
1/4	teaspoon cream of tartar
2	cups light mayonnaise
1/2	teaspoon Worcestershire sauce
48	Ritz Crackers

Instructions

Preheat broiler to high.

Flake the tuna and place in a large bowl.

Beat the egg whites and cream of tartar until stiff. Stir the mayo and worchestershire sauce into the tuna. Fold in the egg whites. Spread on crackers and place on ungreased cookie sheet.

Broil under preheated broiler until puffed.

Serves: 8.

Zucchini Saltimbocca

Recipe Notes

To test the temperature of the oil, place the handle end of a wooden spoon in the oil and when there is serious bubbling around the handle, the oil is ready for frying.

3	medium zucchini, about 2 inches thick and 6-7 inches long
8	slices prosciutto, thinly sliced
8	slices fontina cheese, thinly sliced
1/2	cup flour
1	teaspoon salt
1/2	teaspoon black pepper, freshly ground
1/8	teaspoon cayenne pepper
2	egg whites
1	egg
1	cup panko bread crumbs
4	tablespoons canola oil
1/2	lemon
1	teaspoon Sea Salt

Instructions

Slice the zucchini lengthwise into 16 strips. Place a slice of prosciutto on top of half the slices and cover with a slice of fontina. Lay the remainder of the zucchini on top. They will look like sandwiches.

Mix the flour, salt, pepper and cayenne and put in a flat dish.

Beat the egg with egg whites and place in another dish.

The last dish will hold the panko.

Dredge the zucchini stacks in flour, dip in egg and then in Panko to coat completely. Put on waxed paper lined cookie sheet as you work.

Refrigerate for 20 minutes.

Heat the oil in a large skillet over medium heat until hot. Fry the strips for about 3 minutes until brown on one side and then turn and fry second side.

Season with sea salt. Squeeze the lemon on top. Cut into 1 inch pieces and serve.

Serves: 8.

Breads

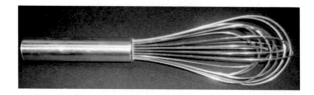

Be sure to have your oven calibrated by your local gas and electric company.
All timing is approximate because ovens cook differently.

Soft Pretzels, p, 43

Cheese Muffins by Mrs. Betteley, p. 40

Butter Dip Biscuits from Mrs. Warren, p. 39

Seasame Tea Bread, p. 42

Butter Dip Biscuits from Mrs. Warren

Recipe Notes

Years ago, we met Mrs. Warren on a Thanksgiving stay on her farm. These are easy on everything but the calories.

2 1/4	cups flour
1	tablespoon sugar
3 1/2	teaspoons baking powder
1 1/2	teaspoons salt
1	cup milk
1	stick butter

Instructions

Preheat oven to 350°.

Sift the flour, sugar, baking powder and salt into a medium bowl. Stir in the milk until just moistened.

Melt butter in 9 x 11 or 8 X 8 baking pan.

Form spoonfuls of dough gently into rounds and drop into the butter, turn to coat evenly with the butter. You can use two fork to do this.
Spoon some butter over the tops to make sure they are coated. Leave in the baking pan and place in oven.

Bake 30 minutes until done.

Makes 9.

Cheese Muffins by Mrs. Betteley

Recipe Notes

Just when you thought you couldn't bake along come a recipe that makes you a star. Just don't work the batter too much or will toughen the muffins. This recipe goes back to an old friend, Judy Betteley, in my Syracuse days.

1	cup flour
2	teaspoons baking powder, fresh
1/2	teaspoon salt
2	tablespoons unsalted butter
1/2	heaping cup sharp cheddar cheese, shredded
1/2	cup milk

Instructions

Preheat oven to 375°.

Sift the flour, baking powder and salt in a medium sized bowl.

Using a hand pastry blender, cut in the butter and then the cheese to the flour until small pieces the size of peas are formed. Add enough milk to moisten. Do not over work the dough. Grease muffin tins or spray with non-stick spray. Use a small ice cream scoop to make all the muffins the same size. Fill cups 3/4 full.

Bake for 30 minutes. Turn onto rack to cool.

Makes 4 large or 8 small or 12 mini

Coconut Tea Bread

Recipe Notes
As a part of a basket of breads for a brunch table, this is a winner! One quarter cup of small pieces of dried pineapple and 1 tsp. rum extract makes this a pinacolada bread....or maybe some chocolate chips for a tropical pain au chocolate...hmmmmm

3	cups flour, sifted
1	tablespoon baking powder
1/2	teaspoon salt
1	cup sugar
1	cup shredded coconut
1	egg, beaten
1	cup milk (for more coconut flavor, use coconut milk)
1	teaspoon vanilla

Instructions

Preheat oven to 350°.

Spray a 9 x 5 x 3 loaf pan with non-stick cooking spray.

Sift the dry ingredients into a medium bowl and add coconut.

Combine the liquid ingredients in a measuring cup and stir into dry ingredients. Blend to combine. Do not over mix! Let stand for 20 minutes. Pour into prepared pan and bake 45-50 minutes until toothpick inserted into center, comes out clean.

Let cool in pan on a rack for 30 minutes. Unmold the bread to slice.

Makes 1 loaf

Sesame Tea Bread

Recipe Notes
This bread is a natural for tea sandwiches. Thinly slice it and spread with a flavorful mixture of dates, walnuts and cream cheese.

3	cups all-purpose flour, sifted
1	teaspoon salt
2 1/2	teaspoons baking powder
1/2	cup sesame seed, toasted until lightly browned
2/3	cup sugar
1/2	cup butter blend, softened
2	eggs
1	teaspoon lemon rind, grated
1 1/2	cups milk
1	tablespoon sesame seed

Instructions

Preheat oven to 350°. Grease and lightly flour a 9x5x3 loaf pan.

Sift flour, salt and baking powder together and mix in the toasted sesame seed in a large bowl.

Combine the sugar and butterblend in work bowl of food processor and process together until light and fluffy, about 15 seconds. Add the eggs and process about 10 seconds. Add lemon rind and milk and process 10 seconds. Add the contents of the processor to the flour all at once and mix until blended, until all the flour streaks are gone, about 40 strokes. Turn into loaf pan. Sprinkle with untoasted sesame seeds.

Bake one 1 and 10 minutes. Test with a toothpick in center. If it comes out wet, bake another 5 minutes.

Cool on a rack for 20 minutes and then unmold.

Serve with a fruit butter: Mix three tbsps. mashed frsh strawberries with 1 Tbsp. confecctioners sugar. Stir into 4 Tbsps.softened butter mixed with 4 Tbsps. whipped cream cheese.

Makes 1 loaf

Soft Pretzels

Recipe Notes
You could add all sorts of different toppings: sesame seeds, poppy seeds, cinnamon and sugar or whatever else you can think of. You can mix mustard into the egg mixture...think of the possibilities.

These are an easy treat to make with Girl Scouts or on a rainy day with the kids.

1 1/2	cups warm water
1	package dry yeast
1	tablespoon sugar
1/8	teaspoon powdered ginger
1	teaspoon salt
4	cups all-purpose flour
1	egg, beaten
1/4	cup large crystal salt

Instructions

Preheat oven to 425°.

Pour warm water and yeast into work bowl of food processor and process 10 seconds.

Pour off into a large measuring cup. Return the work bowl to the base and put in flour, sugar, ginger, and salt. Pour in 1/2 cup yeast mixture and start processing. Add the remaining liquid quickly down the feeding tube. Turn off after all the liquid is in. Scrape down the sides of the bowl and process until a ball forms. If too dry add about 1-2 tablespoons water. Remove the dough and place in a bowl and cover with a cloth. Let rest 30 minutes. Remove from the bowl and shape into a long log. Cut into 16 equal pieces. Roll each piece into a rope about 21 inches long. Form into a "u" shape with the bottom of the "u" facing you. Take the ends and twist twice. Bring the ends back to you and place on the bottom of the "u". Brush each with beaten egg and sprinkle with salt. Place on a lightly greased cookie sheet and bake for 15 minutes until brown.

Serve warm or at room temperature. If making in advance, freeze and then heat to thaw.

Makes 16 small

Salad

Make a large bowl of a salad base. Cover tightly and it will be good for three to four days. Add new ingredients each night to vary the taste of each new menu.

Salade Nicoise, p. 53

Caesar Salad, p. 47

Spinach Salad, p.54

Caesar Salad

Recipe Notes

Forty five years have elapsed since I learned this recipe from a friend named Mary Peterson in Syracuse. She was a Texan and this recipe has never changed except the raw eggs are gone.

To dry large amounts of torn Romaine lettuce, double bag in cottom pillow cases and put in **clothes washer on spin.** ***Not the dryer!****The cases will absorb the water. You can then roll the leaves in dishtowels and place in plastic bag until making the salad .*

2	pounds romaine lettuce
1	pound Pepperidge Farm sliced white bread
3/4	cup garlic oil*
2	lemons
1/4	cup red wine vinegar
1/2	cup Eggbeaters
1	teaspoon dry mustard powder
1	teaspoon Worcestershire sauce
10	anchovies, mashed
1/2	cup canola oil
1	cup Grated Parmesan Cheese

Instructions

Wash and dry lettuce. Break into bite size pieces and chill.

To make the croutons:

Trim crust of the white bread and slice into 16 cubes per slice.

Turn oven on to its lowest setting. Place croutons on a cookie sheet and place in oven. Fluff the croutons every half hour for about 2 1/2 to 3 hours until dried completely. If not golden brown, turn oven up to 350° and WATCH LIKE A HAWK- because they will burn- until golden.

3 hours before serving: Fill a quart container with croutons and add 3/4 cup of garlic oil and invert jar every half hour until totally absorbed by the croutons.

*Press or minced about 8 serious garlic cloves into 3/4 C canola oil and let sit over night. Strain out the oil before using.

Dressing:

Mix the juice of two fresh lemons with enough red wine vinegar to measure 1/2 cup.

Add Eggbeaters eguivalent to 2 eggs and mix in 1 teaspoon dry mustard and 1 teaspoon Worcestershire sauce. Mash anchovies in the bottom of a large bowl. Add the lettuce, egg mixture and oil. Top with croutons and grated cheese. Toss and serve.

Serves: 8. Serves 12-16 on a buffet.

Corn and Black Bean Salad

Recipe Notes
This recipe can be made with either fresh or frozen corn depending on the season.

Great for a summer buffet but with the frozen corn, it could be an anytime dish. Good side dish for a dinner of enchiladas or tacos.

1/3	cup rice vinegar
1/4	cup olive oil
2	tablespoons lime juice
4	corn on cob **or**
2	cups frozen corn
4	cups canned black beans, rinsed & drained
1/2	cup red onion, finely chopped
1	green pepper, cored and diced
1	red bell pepper, cored and diced
1/3	cup cilantro, finely chopped
1	teaspoon salt and pepper

Instructions

Whisk together the vinegar, olive oil, lime juice, salt and pepper in a small bowl until blended. Set dressing aside.

Bring 4 cups of salted water to a boil in a small pot over high heat. Add corn and cook for 1 minute. Drain and rinse corn well in cold water to stop the cooking, then drain again. Cut kernels from cobs into bowl. (If using frozen corn, bring water to a boil, drop in the frozen corn and cook 3-4 minutes and drain well.)

Add the beans, onions and bell peppers to the bowl and toss to mix. Add the reserved dressing to the bean mixture and gently toss until just incorporated.   Cover and refrigerate for about 2 hours. Add cilantro, salt and pepper to taste, and toss again before serving.

Serves: 8.

Deluxe Potato Salad

Recipe Notes
A beautiful dish to add to the tailgate spread because there is no mayo, it's good to travel.

3	eggs, hard boiled
6	slices bacon, cooked
1	cup olive oil
1/2	cup white wine vinegar
1	teaspoon dijon mustard
1/2	teaspoon freshly ground black pepper
1 1/2	teaspoons salt
4	cups potatoes
2	tablespoons pimientos, chopped
6	chopped anchovy fillets, optional
1	large romaine lettuce
1/2	cup scallions, sliced
1/2	cup Parmesan cheese, shredded

Instructions
Slice the hard boiled eggs into wedges.

Cook the bacon on paper towel in microwave covered for three minutes on high. Check after two and one half minutes to see if they are crisp.
Remove, crumble, and set aside.

Dressing: Beat together olive oil, white wine vinegar, salt and fresh ground pepper.

Cook the potatoes. Peel and dice into 1" cubes.

Pour half the dressing over the warm potatoes and save the remainder. Mix the pimentos and anchovies with potatoes. Cover and chill. Stir potatoes several times while they chill.

Line a large salad bowl with some of the outer romaine leaves. Break the remainder of the head in bite sized pieces and place in bowl. Cover with cold potato mixture.

Arrange sliced eggs, scallions and parmesan over the potatoes and sprinkle the crumbled bacon over all.

Serves: 8.

Mayonnaise- Blender made

Recipe Notes
It is so easy to make really good mayo you may do it all the time.
If you have anyone that might have a problem with the raw egg, than use a very good store bought brand instead.

1	egg
1	tablespoon lemon juice
1/2	teaspoon salt
1/2	teaspoon dry mustard powder
3/4	cup canola oil

Instructions

Put the egg, lemon juice,salt and mustard into a blender. Turn the blender on low speed and add about 3 tablespoons of the oil. Then pour the rest of the oil in very slowly in a slow steam. Should be smooth and creamy in less than a minute.

Makes about 1 cup

Mother of all Salads

Recipe Notes
*The dressing is the secret... put it on anything fresh and you will have a great salad.
The idea is any lettuce, with any cheese, with any fruit and any nut to make a different salad every time.*

1	package salad greens
1/4	cup blue cheese
1	cup Fruit (mango, pear, apple, grapefruit, etc), diced
1	cup cherry tomato
4	tablespoons Nuts (pecans, pignolis, slivered almonds, waltnuts, etc)

Instructions

Use any bagged salad or make a selection of baby greens.

DRESSING:

1 Tbsp. Dijon Mustard
1/2 cup Seasoned Rice Wine Vinegar (the kind with the sugar in it.)
3 Tbsp. water
1/3 cup canola oil

Beat mustard and vinegar together then add water and mix again. Pour in oil and beat or shake until blended.

Toss salad in large bowl and add 1/3 cup dressing and toss again. If you need more dressing add slowly and toss agin. Season with salt and pepper.

Serves: 8.

Rice Salad

Recipe Notes
There comes a time when you need another salad for the buffet.
This is it...and it is able to withstand the weather on a hot summer day if kept on an ice bed. Even though it has no mayo, rice can spoil if left in the heat too long.

1 1/2	cups rice
3	cloves garlic
1	teaspoon salt
1/8	teaspoon pepper
1	teaspoon dry mustard powder
3/4	cup olive oil
6	tablespoons rice wine vinegar
1	medium onion, sliced thinly
4	large tomatoes, sliced in chunks
2	pimientos, cut in strips
1/2	cup parsley, minced

Instructions

Cook the rice as directed on the package. The 1 1/2 cups of dry rice should give you 3 cups of cooked rice. Chill rice.

Mash the garlic in a bowl and add salt, pepper, mustard and oil. Beat to mix well. Add the vinegar, onion, tomatoes and pimentos. Marinate until serving. Before serving toss with rice and parsley.

Serves: 8.

Salade Nicoise

<u>Recipe Notes</u>
You can use all sorts of fresh ingredients with canned fish, olives, and anchovies. You will have a new version each time.
Of course, you can leave out the anchovies if no one likes them.

1	bag of mixed salad greens
1 1/2	pounds small new potatoes
2	pounds string beans, trimmed and cut into 2" lengths
1	red onion, sliced thin
8	ounces pitted black olives, drained
1	pint cherry tomato
8	hard boiled eggs, shelled & quartered
2	8 oz. cans tuna, drained
1	can Flat anchovies, drained (optional)

Instructions
Chopped the lettuce for serving.

Cover the potaotes with cold salted water, bring to a boil and simmer about 10 minutes until tender but still firm enough to slice. Cool and slice or cut in cubes.

In another large pot of salted boiling water, cook the beans uncovered for 5 minutes. Pour the beans in a colander and run cold water on them until they are cool.

Pile lettuce greens on a large flat serving bowl. In a large mixing bowl combine the potatoes, beans, onions and olives with 1/2 cup dressing. place the mixture on top of the greens. Put tomatoes and eggs around the edge of the bowl. Crumble the tuna over the top and crisscross the anchovies over the tuna. Pour the remaining dressing over all.

Dressing:
1 Tbsp. Dijion mustard
4 Tbsp. red wine vinegar
1 tsp. granulated sugar
1 tsp. salt
fresh ground pepper
1/2 cup extra virgin olive oil

Put the mustard in a small bowl and then whisk in the vinegar, sugar, salt and pepper. Add oil and mix again.

Serves: 8.

Spinach Salad

Recipe Notes
If you add quartered hard cooked eggs, this is a full lunch meal.

6	slices bacon, crumbled
1	pound tender young spinach
2	tablespoons bacon fat, reserved
1	cup stale bread croutons
1	medium red onion
1/2	cup olive oil
2	tablespoons red wine vinegar
1/2	teaspoon salt
2	pinches fresh pepper
1/4	teaspoon dry mustard powder

Instructions

Fry the bacon until crisp. Crumble. Place bacon on paper towel and reserve bacon fat.

Wash and dry the spinach. When spinach is dry, tear or cut into shreds. Set aside.

Heat the reserved fat in a medium skillet and saute the croutons until golden and crisp. Set aside.

Slice onion in thin slices. Set aside.

In a salad bowl, blend the oil, vinegar, salt, pepper and mustard vigorously. Add spinach and toss. Add bacon, croutons and onions. Toss Again.

Serves: 6.

Soups

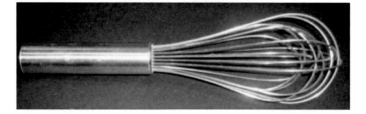

Make more soup than you need and freeze for a time you don't want to cook.
A salad and bread will round out a meal.

Curried Butternut Squash with Apples Soup, p. 60

Tomato Soup-Shhhhhh, p. 67

Onion Soup, p. 64

Chilled Minted Pea Soup, p. 58

Bisque of Whatever Soup

<u>Recipe Notes</u>
WHATEVER is whatever you have in the vegetable drawer ie:
zucchini, carrots, turnips, broccoli, greens, parsnip...you get the idea.
The only thing I don't use is beets because they change the color of the soup.
The important part is adding the potato to thicken the mixture.
If you wish to leave out the cream, add a little more broth to get the texture you like.

2	pounds whatever
1	medium onion
2	medium potatoes
1/4	teaspoon marjoram, dried
1/4	teaspoon rosemary, crushed
1	quart chicken broth
1 1/2	teaspoons salt
1/4	teaspoon cayenne pepper
1/2	cup heavy cream

Instructions

Chop the whatever in small pieces and pulse in the food processor then put in 4 quart pot. You may have to do batches. Add the broth, potatoes, onion and spices. Simmer until the veggies are soft.

Puree in food mill or blender (be careful when blending hot liquids in blender. DO NOT OVERLOAD!)

Return the mixture to the pot...(strain if you want it very smooth).

Season with salt and cayenne.

Heat until bubblling and then reduce the heat and add the cream. Stir gently, do not boil . When heated, serve.

You can garnish with canned french fried onions or snipped chives.

Serves: 6.

Chilled Minted Sweet Pea Soup

Recipe Notes
To change the soup you might add pea shoots (available in Chinese markets) instead of the mint and garnish with lump crab meat for a filling lunch or fancy starter to a formal dinner.

1	tablespoon butter
1	cup onion, chopped
2	pounds frozen peas
3/4	cup fresh mint
1	quart chicken stock
1	dash cayenne pepper
1	teaspoon salt
1/2	teaspoon black pepper
1	cup fat free half and half
6	tablespoons creme fraiche

Instructions

Melt butter in a large pot and sauté onion until wilted but not brown. Add the peas, mint and the chicken stock and bring to a boil. Season with cayenne, salt and pepper. Simmer for ten minutes. Let cool for 15 minutes then blend in batches in the blender or food mill. Pass each batch through a sieve into a large bowl. Add the cup of half and half and chill at least four hours.

To serve:

Fill a tea cup with soup and top with a teaspoon of creme fraiche and a half teaspoon of caviar if desired.

Serves: 6.

Corn Chowder

<u>Recipe Notes</u>
*You can use this as a base for any chowder. Add chopped clams or crab meat...(at college, they would use canned tuna for Sunday night supper...you **don't** want to do this!) Lobster is nice if you feel flush.*

By adding more veggies you can have a dinner that is filling and nutritious.

1	tablespoon unsalted butter
3	slices Canadian bacon, chopped
1	large onion, chopped
1	red pepper, diced fine
4	yukon gold potato, 1/2 inch cubes
6	cups chicken broth
2	cups water
3	cups corn, frozen
1	teaspoon salt
1/2	teaspoon pepper, freshly ground
1	pinch cayenne pepper
2	cups cream

Instructions

Melt butter in a large pot over medium heat and then add the bacon. Cook until limp but not browned; add the onions and red pepper. Stir until wilted and then add the potatoes, chicken broth and water.

Bring to a boil and then simmer for 15 minutes, until potatoes are just tender. Remove 3 cups of the solids to a bowl and blend with motor stick or in blender until smooth. Be careful when blending hot liquids in blender to not over fill. Return to the pot.

Add the corn, salt and pepper.......taste to adjust the seasonings and add cayenne. Taste again. Simmer 8-10 minutes to cook the corn. Add the cream and just heat through, **DO NOT BOIL**.

Serves: 6.

Curried Butternut Squash with Apples Soup

<u>Recipe Notes</u>
A robust winter soup that warms more than just your cockles. Top with a little creme fraiche if you like.

1	tablespoon olive oil
1	large onion, finely chopped
1	tablespoon curry powder
1	large butternut squash, peeled & cubed
4	large apples, peeled and quartered
1	quart chicken broth
1/8	cup toasted pumpkin or squash seeds

Instructions

Use tart apples like Granny Smiths.

Heat oil in a deep heavy pot. Sauté onion until limp but not brown. Stir in curry powder and stir until completely incorporated with the onions. Add the squash and the apples and pour in the chicken stock. Bring to a boil and simmer about 30 minutes until very soft.

Blend with motor stick or in the blender (be careful when blending hot liquids..do a little at a time!) If it is too thick, add water and if too thin reduce by simmering a little while longer.

Put into a bowl or demi-tasse cups. Top with pumpkin seeds as garnish.

Serves: 8.

Egg Drop Soup

Recipe Notes
Snow peas or pea shoots are a great addition.
Faster than having it delivered!

1	quart chicken broth
1	tablespoon soy sauce
1	tablespoon cornstarch
3	tablespoons water
2	scallions, chopped
1/2	teaspoon sesame oil

Instructions

Lightly beat the eggs with 2 Tablespoons of water.

Bring the broth to a boil. Reduce the heat to simmer. Stir in the soy sauce. Combine the cornstarch and water in a small bowl and stir to dissolve. Add the cornstarch to the soup and stir until thickened. Simmer over low heat for two minutes.

Re-beat the eggs and slowly add to the simmering broth. Turn off the heat and stir in scallions. Add 1/2 tsp. sesame oil if desired.

Serves: 2.

Grandma Sylvia's Spinach Soup

Recipe Notes
As a child, this was my favorite breakfast instead of hot cereal.

4	large baking potatoes
2	boxes frozen chopped spinach
4	ounces unsalted butter
1	cup milk, warm
1	teaspoon salt
1	teaspoon pepper

Instructions

Bake potatoes 1 hour at 350° or until done.

Prepare the spinach as package directs. No need to drain.

Scoop out the potatoes and reserve the skins for stuffed skins. Put the milk in blender and add the spinach, potatoes, butter and seasonings. Blend, adding extra milk until reaching desired consistancy. Should be like thick creamed spinach or heavy oatmeal.

Serves: 6.

Minestrone

Recipe Notes
The bacon is a really good addition to any soup. You can use Pancetta if it is available. If you don't have one of the vegetables, leave it out...it will be a great soup. anyway.

1	cup string beans, fresh
1	teaspoon olive oil
1/8	pound bacon, chopped
1	clove garlic, chopped
1	onion, chopped
1	teaspoon parsley, chopped
1	tablespoon tomato paste
1	cup water
1	teaspoon salt
1/2	teaspoon freshly ground black pepper
3	stalks celery, diced
2	carrots, sliced
2	potatoes, cubed
1	can cannellini beans
1/2	head cabbage, shredded
1	cup elbow macaroni, cooked al dente
1/2	cup Grated Parmesan Cheese
2	quarts chicken broth

Instructions

Cut fresh string beans into 1 inch pieces.

In large soup pot heat the oil and add bacon. Cook until wilted- DO NOT BROWN! Add garlic, onion and parsley. Simmer 5 minutes.

Dissolve tomato paste in 1 cup of water. Add dissolved tomato paste, salt, pepper, celery, carrots, potatoes, string beans and cannelini beans to the soup pot. Simmer for 2 minutes.

Add chicken broth and bring to a boil. Simmer for 1/2 hour.

Add cabbage and macaroni and simmer for 10 minutes. Add cheese and simmer an additional 10 minutes. Pour into a large tureen and serve into soup bowls with fresh crusty bread. Pass extra cheese if you like.

Serves: 8.

Onion Soup

Recipe Notes
Buy yourself a set of soup crocks that can go under the broiler.
You can put all soups in them and they really look good.

Presentation, Presentation, Presentation!!!

1	loaf French bread
1 1/2	pounds onions, sliced
3	tablespoons butter
1	tablespoon olive oil
1/2	teaspoon sugar
1	tablespoon salt
3	tablespoons flour
1	quart water, boiling
1	quart beef broth
2	cups gruyere, shredded

Instructions

Slice french bread and toast. The bread is better a little stale.

Thinly slice the onions. In large soup pot, heat the butter and oil, add the onions and cook over low heat 15 minutes covered. Uncover and raise heat to medium; stir in sugar and salt. Cook for 30 minutes until deep, golden brown.

Sprinkle in flour, cook for 3 minutes. Add stock and water and boil for another 20 minutes.

Preheat oven to 350°.

Spoon very hot soup into crocks, place as many pieces of toast as it takes to cover the top; cover heaily with grated cheese. Bake for 15 minutes, then slip under the broiler to brown top slightly.

Serves: 6.

Peanut Soup

Recipe Notes
Just try it!....It is delicious and kids will love it. A great nutitional meal with a cheese sandwich.

4	tablespoons unsalted butter
1	medium onion, chopped
2	stalks celery, chopped
3 1/2	tablespoons flour
2	quarts chicken broth
1/2	pint Creamy Peanut Butter
1 1/2	teaspoons salt
1	Juice of one lemon
1	ounce Roasted Peanuts, chopped small
3	ounces peanuts

Instructions

Melt butter in a 3 quart pot. Add the onions and celery and cook over medium heat until wilted, about 10 minutes. Do not brown! Add the flour and stir until thick and all butter is absorbed. Slowly add the chicken stock, keep stirring until it boils.

Pour the soup through a medium strainer into a large bowl. Return the soup to the pot and add the peanut butter. Stir with a wooden spoon until completely melted into soup. When totally heated, add chopped peanuts, laddle into bowls and garnish with a teaspoon of peanuts in each serving.

Serves: 8.

Remy's Mushroom Soup

Recipe Notes
*My granddaughter, Remy, loves mushrooms and onions. This recipe includes them both.
Even though it has a long list of ingredients, it is so much better than anything that ever came
in a can. Try it once and this soup will be the starter for many dinners to come.*

1 1/2	pounds mixed mushrooms, shitake,portobella, button etc.
2	tablespoons olive oil
1	cup onion, chopped
1	teaspoon dried thyme
1	teaspoon Sea Salt
1/4	teaspoon cayenne pepper
1 1/2	quarts water
6	tablespoons unsalted butter
2	cups leeks, chopped fine
6	tablespoons flour
1	teaspoon black pepper, freshly ground
2	cups half and half
1/4	cup fresh parsley, chopped
1	cup dry white wine
1	tablespoon Sea Salt
1/2	teaspoon cayenne pepper
4	tablespoons fresh chives, chopped

Instructions

Fill a large bowl with cold water and submerge the chopped leeks. Squish around in the water to release any dirt. Lift the leeks gently out of the water to a colander to drain.

Wipe the mushrooms with a damp cloth to remove any loose dirt. Remove the stems and chop them. Slice the caps and set aside.

Heat the olive oil in a large pot. Add the mushrooms stems, onions, dried thyme, salt and cayenne. Cook over low heat until onions are soft but not brown. Add the water, bring to a boil and then simmer for 20 minutes. Pour through a fine strainer into a large bowl and discard the solids. If needed, add enough water to make 6 cups. Reserve.

Rinse and dry the large pot and melt the butter. When the butter is foaming, add the leeks and cook until soft about 15 minutes. Add the reserved sliced mushroom caps and cook until soft, another 10 minutes. Stir in the flour until completely incorporated. Add the wine and stir until it is completely mixed. Add the reserved mushroom broth, salt and cayenne. Bring to a boil, reduce the heat and simmer for 15 minutes. Add the half and half and parsley and heat through but do not boil.

Top each soup bowl with chopped chives and serve hot.

Serves: 6

Secret Tomato Soup, Shhhhh!

Recipe Notes
You can serve this in demi-tasse cups as an appetizer or as a buffet offering.

3	cans Condensed Tomato Soup
1	box Pomi chopped tomatoes
1	cup fresh basil, chopped
3	cups milk

Instructions

Combine the soup, tomatoes and milk in a large sauce pan. When hot, but not boiling, add basil; ladle into cups. Top each cup with a dollop of creme fraiche or sour cream. Garnish with basil leaf.

Serves: 6.

Pasta and Grains

Everyone loves a starch! Try different shapes of pasta with steamed veggies,

a little olive oil and a few herbs as a simple, healthy dinner.

Alec's Macaroni and Cheese, p. 71

Capellini with Clam Sauce, p. 73

Linguine with Zucchini, p. 77

Kasha Varnitchkes, p. 75

Alec's Mac and Cheese

<u>Recipe Notes</u>
This is my grandson Alec's favorite food!

Truly it is one of everyone's favorite foods....you can add all kinds of meats or seafood or veggies to make this every day.

Don't have elbows?....How about penne or fusilli?

This could be a book all itself....just use the basics and add what you like.

1	pound elbow macaroni, cooked al dente
2	tablespoons flour
2	tablespoons unsalted butter
1	teaspoon dry mustard powder
1/2	teaspoon paprika
1	teaspoon salt
1/2	teaspoon pepper, freshly ground
2	cups milk
2	cups sharp cheddar cheese
1/2	cup sharp cheddar cheese

Instructions

Preheat oven to 350°.

Cook the macaroni, drain and set aside. Mix the flour with the mustard, paprika, salt and pepper.

Heat a large skillet over moderate heat. Melt the butter and when it is foamy add the flour mixture and stir with a whisk until all the lumps are gone. Add the milk and cook until it is smooth and thick.

Stir in 2 cups of cheddar cheese and stir until thoroughly melted. Stir in the cooked macaroni until it is all coated with the cheese.

Turn into a greased 2 quart casserole, cover with foil and bake for 20 minutes. Uncover, sprinkle with remaining cheddar, return to oven and baked uncovered for about 10 minutes more until brown and bubbling.

Serves: 6.

Barley Casserole

Recipe Notes
Barley is really a neglected grain. Not a bad side dish for all red meat.
Add some greens and change the chicken stock to vegetable and it is a vegetarian
entree. A good alternative to potatoes.

2	tablespoons olive oil
2	tablespoons unsalted butter
1	cup onion, chopped
1	pound mushrooms, sliced
1 1/2	cups barley
2	pimientos, chopped
2	cups chicken stock, boiling
1	teaspoon salt
1/2	teaspoon black pepper, freshly ground

Instructions

Preheat oven to 350°.

Heat oil and the butter in a 3 quart saucepan, stir in the onions and mushrooms and cook until the mushrooms are tender.

Add the barley and cook the mixture until barley is lightly browned. Transfer the mixture to an oven proof casserole. Add the pimento and the chicken stock. Add salt and pepper to taste. Cover the casserole with lid or foil and bake for 50-60 minutes or until barley in tender and the liquid is absorbed.

Stir several times during the baking and if at any time it seems dry, add some extra water or stock.

Serves: 8.

Capellini with Clam Sauce

Recipe Notes
*You can purchase chopped clams by the pint in fresh fish markets.
By all means, use the fresh chopped clams when possible.*

Do not use dried parsley ever! Leave it out if you don't have fresh.

6	cloves garlic, minced (more is better)
1/4	cup olive oil
1/2	teaspoon red pepper flakes
2	cans clams, chopped (fresh chopped when available)
1	tablespoon fresh parsley, chopped
1	teaspoon dried oregano
1	pound cappellini, cooked al dente

Instructions

Cook the pasta al dente and drain reserving one and one half cups of cooking liquid.

Heat oil over moderate heat in a large skillet. Add the garlic and cook until golden. **DO NOT BURN!** Add the red pepper flakes and the clams and heat through. Stir in the parsley and oregano; add the reserved cup of pasta water.   Add the cappellini to the skillet and stir to mix with clams and heat the pasta. Serve in warmed bowls.

Serves: 4.

Homemade Rice-a-Roni

Recipe Notes
So GOOD without all the preservatives!!

Add veggies for a vegetarian main dish...just add cooked vegetables in any amounts.

Color counts for nutrition and presentation.

The only vegetable I serve on its own is beets because they bleed their color into the recipe.

4	tablespoons butter
1	ounce vermicelli or capellini, broken in 1/2 inch pieces
2	cups rice, uncooked
5	cups chicken broth, boiling
1	teaspoon salt

Instructions

Melt butter in a large skillet. Add the vermicelli and stir until lightly browned.

Add the rice and stir to coat with the butter. Add the boiling broth and salt. Cover, reduce the heat and simmer about 20 minutes until liquid is absorbed.

If not absorbed cook a little longer, stirring once or twice.

Serves: 6.

Kasha Varnitchkes

Recipe Notes
Kasha is a really healthy grain. It is earthy in flavor and gluten free.

1/2	cup canola oil
1	large onion, diced
1 1/2	cups buckwheat groats (Kasha)
2	eggs
3	cups water, boiling
1	teaspoon salt
1	pound Bowtie (Farfalle) pasta, cooked al dente

Instructions

Pour the oil over the onions in a medium skillet and place over medium heat. Cover the pan and sweat the onions until they release their liquid. Uncover, lower the heat, and cook until the onions are golden brown. Remove from the heat and set aside.

In a large pot, combine the Kasha with the eggs and place over medium heat. Stir constantly, cook the Kasha until it is brown and the grains are separate and smell toasted.

Add the boiling water and salt and cook covered over medium heat for 10-15 minutes until the water is absorbed. The grains should be tender and about doubled in bulk.

Add four tablespoons of the onions with their oil. Stir to coat all the grains.

Stir together with the bowtie pasta.

Serves: 4.

Lasagna for a Crowd

Recipe Notes
Traditional lasagna for a great party with a salad and garlic bread.
To make half... make all the sauce. Use half the amount of the other ingredients. Use one pound of noodles and freeze the remaining sauce.

2	pounds ground beef, lean
1	pound sausage, hot or sweet Italian
2	cups onions, chopped
3	cloves garlic, minced
32	ounces tomato sauce
3	cups water
2	tablespoons tomato paste
1	cup red wine
1	teaspoon basil, dried
1	teaspoon oregano, dried
2	bay leaves
3	pounds ricotta cheese
1	pound mozzarella, shredded
1	cup Parmesan cheese, grated
2	boxes no cook lasagne nookles

Instructions

Traditional lasagna for a great party with a salad and garlic bread.

Prepare two 9 X 13 pans by spraying with nonstick spray.

Heat a large skillet over medium heat and add meat and sausage. Stir until no pink remains and then add the onions and garlic. Brown the meat and wilt the onions. Drain off fat by pouring into a colander. Place the meat in a large pot and add all the other ingredients except the noodles and cheeses. Cook the sauce about 1 1/2 hours until thick...add a little extra water if too thick. Set aside.

Preheat oven to 350°.
To assemble:
Prepare two 9X13 pans with non stick spray.
Coat the bottom of each pan with a layer of sauce. Remove noodles from box and lay side by side in pan to make a layer. Spoon on sauce, a layer of meat and then some ricotta and sprinkle with mozzarella. Repeat the process and then top with noodles, mozzarella, and parmesan. Spray foil with nonstick spray and cover. Bake for 30 minutes, uncover and bake until brown and bubbly, about 15 minutes more.
Serves: 8.

Linguine with Zucchini

Recipe Notes
When you don't know what to do with all that Zucchini that is coming in from the garden...this is it. Or maybe make the Zucchini Saltimboca.

1	pound linguine
2	large zucchini, julienned (cut in long narrow strips)
1	teaspoon Sea Salt
1	tablespoon olive oil
2	cloves garlic, minced
1/2	teaspoon red pepper flakes
1	tablespoon fresh basil, chopped
1	tablespoon fresh parsley, chopped
	Parmesan cheese

Instructions

Place the zucchini in a large colander. Sprinkle with salt and weight down with a plate and heavy can. Leave for 20 minutes to drain. Rinse and dry with clean dish towel.

Bring 6 quarts of water to a boil add 1 Tbsp. salt and cook pasta al dente as box directs. Reserve 1 1/2 cups of cooking liquid. Drain pasta.

Heat olive oil in a large skillet. Saute garlic until golden add the red pepper flakes, stir for one minute and add the zucchini. Stir until zucchini is wilted and add the reserved pasta water, linguine, basil and parsley. Serve in a warmed bowl. Pass the Parmesan cheese.

Serves: 4.

Pasta with Garlic and Oil

Recipe Notes

This is a fast dinner for real garlic lovers. Add steamed broccoli florets or steamed broccoli rabe for a switch.

1	pound spaghetti
1	tablespoon kosher salt
1/4	cup olive oil
1	tablespoon garlic, chopped
3	tablespoons parsley, chopped
4	ounces unsalted butter
1/4	teaspoon red pepper flakes

Instructions

Bring a large pot of water to a boil. Add the salt and spaghetti and cook as box directs for al dente. Save 1 1/2 cups of pasta cooking water. Drain.

Heat a large skillet over medium heat. Add the olive oil and butter and heat until butter foams. Add the garlic, parsley and red pepper flakes. Cook over medium heat until garlic is golden. Add the pasta to the skillet and toss to coat. Add reserved pasta water if needed for extra moisture.

Serves: 4.

Penne with Sausage and Fennel

<u>Recipe Notes</u>
If you would like to leave out the sausage and make it taste as though it were still there....add a tablespoon of ground fennel seeds.

1	pound sausage, hot or sweet Italian
1/2	cup red wine
1	tablespoon olive oil
3	cloves garlic, minced
1	head fennel bulb
1/2	teaspoon red pepper flakes
1	pound penne, cooked al dente
2	tablespoons fresh basil, chiffonade (cut in thin shreds)
1/2	cup Parmesan cheese, grated

Instructions

Be sure to save1 1/2 cups of pasta water when you drain the pasta.

Cut the fennel bulb in half from top to bottom. Slice across the bulb into thin slices. Set aside.

Pierce the sausages with a knife in several places. Heat a large skillet over medium heat. Cook the sausages until brown on all sides. Add the wine to the skillet and cook the sausages for about 10 minutes until cooked through. Remove and slice on the diagonal in one inch pieces. Wipe out the skillet and heat the oil. Saute the garlic until wilted and then add the fennel and red pepper flakes. Saute until the fennel is lightly browned. Add the sausage back to the skillet. Add the reserved pasta water and then the penne. Lastly, stir in the basil and serve in warmed bowls.

Pass Parmesan cheese.

Serves: 4.

Poultry

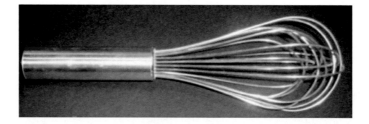

Use care when working with raw poultry. Be sure to clean your utensils, boards, sink and hands and do not cross contaminate your work areas.

Chicken Savoy, p. 87

Chicken Breast Superb, p. 85
 with Homemade Rice-a-Roni, p. 74

Chicken Piccata, p. 86

Chicken A La Kiev, p.83

Chicken A La Kiev

Recipe Notes
To test the temperature of the oil, place the handle end of a wooden spoon in the oil and when there is serious bubbling around the handle the oil is ready to fry the chicken. You can use the Pistachio- Gorgonzola Torte as a filling and proceed as directed. Barley Casserole and Roasted Root Veggies are good accompaniments. **Serves: 4**.

4	large chicken breasts, boned, halved
10	ounces butter
2	ounces fresh parsley, chopped
12	shallots, chopped, finely
2	cloves garlic, chopped
1 1/4	cups bread crumbs
6	tablespoons Parmesan cheese, grated, finely
1	teaspoon salt
1 1/2	teaspoons black pepper, freshly ground
2	whole eggs
1	cup flour
1/2	cup canola oil

Instructions

Pound chicken between two sheets of waxed paper until it is 1/2 inch thick and even.

Mix together 8 Tbsp. butter, parsley, shallots, garlic, 1/4 cup bread crumbs and parmesan cheese. Roll it into a log with waxed paper and cut into 8 even pieces.

Lay each chicken breast half, skin side down, on wax paper and sprinkle with a little salt and pepper. Place one piece of the butter mixture in the center of each breast. Roll the breast covering the butter mixture completely with the breast. Shape with your hand into an egg roll shape. Beat 2 whole eggs with 2 tablespoons of canola oil. Season the flour with about 1/2 tsp. each of salt and pepper. Set up three dishes with flour in one, eggs in another and the remaining one cup of bread crumbs in the last .

Dip breasts in flour and shake off excess, then in the egg and roll in bread crumbs. Press chicken between hands to make breading adhere and shape uniform. You will not need to tie them. Place in fridge for 1/2 hour.
Preheat oven to 350°.

Heat a medium sized skillet; add the canola oil. Heat over moderate heat until about 350 degrees (see hint). Add the breasts and brown on all sides about 3-5 minutes.

Remove the chicken to a oven proof casserole, dot with the remaining 2 Tbsp. of butter and bake for in preheated oven for 15 minutes.

Chicken Breasts Aloha

Recipe Notes
This can be made and served room temperature on a buffet table.
(Not on a hot summer day.)

4	whole chicken breasts, halved
1	cup coconut milk
1	tablespoon salt
1/2	teaspoon allspice, ground
1/2	cup coconut, shredded
2	eggs
1/2	cup unsalted butter

Instructions

Season the chicken with salt. Use 1/3 of the cup of coconut milk, Allspice and salt to moisten the chicken. Cover and place in fridge for 2 housrs.

Toast the coconut in oven (I use the toaster oven at 350 and watch it carefully) until lightly browned. Beat eggs and mix in the remaining 2/3 cup of coconut milk.
 One half hour before serving, roll the chicken in toasted coconut and set aside. When ready to cook, heat the butter in a large skillet until foaming and bubbling. Dip the chicken pieces in the egg batter and slip into the butter. Cook over medium heat until browned on first side about 10 minutes. Turn and cook about 15 minutes more. Check to make sure it is cooked on inside. If cooking too quickly, reduce heat.

Jasmine Rice and Steamed Broccoli completes this dish.

Serves: 6.

Chicken Breasts Superb

Recipe Notes
Any sharp melting cheese will work great as well. Asiago is a great choice.

6	tablespoons unsalted butter
1/2	pound mushrooms, sliced
6	chicken breasts, split and boned
1/2	cup flour
1/4	teaspoon salt and pepper
6	slices fontina cheese

Instructions

Heat two tablespoons of butter in a large skillet and saute the mushrooms until brown. Remove from the skillet and reserve.

Remove and discard skin from chicken. Place the breasts, skin side down, on board and pound thin between two sheets of waxed paper.

Season the flour with the salt and peper. Dip the chicken breasts in flour on both sides and brush off excess flour. Heat the butter in a large skillet. Add the chicken and cook until tender, five or six minutes on each side. Remove to a shallow broiler proof pan. Arrange a spoonful of cooked mushrooms on each breast of chicken and cover with a slice of cheese.

Place chicken under a hot broiler just long enough to melt the cheese.

Plate and serve with tomato casserole and corn pudding.

Serves: 6.

Chicken Piccata

Recipe Notes
You can used defrosted artichoke hearts instead of canned.

If you don't have open white wine, you can always use dry vermouth.
Keep a bottle around for all your white wine needs...do not use cooking wine from the supermarket...it is loaded with salt and tastes really nasty!

3	lemons
1	cup flour
1	teaspoon salt
1/2	teaspoon pepper
2	pounds chicken breasts, pounded thin
1/2	cup olive oil
1/2	cup white wine
1	can artichoke hearts, sliced, and drained
2	tablespoons capers

Instructions

Juice 2 lemons and set aside. Slice the third lemon thinly and set aside.

Season the flour with the salt and pepper.

Dredge the chicken with seasoned flour. Heat the olive in a large skillet until very hot. Saute chicken for about 2 minutes on each side, or until tender. Remove from pan and keep warm.

Pour off any oil in pan and add wine and lemon juice. Bring the mixture to a boil, stirring and scrapping up all the bits that cling to the pan. Cook sauce until it thickens slightly.

Return chicken the pan and add artichokes, capers and lemon slices.   Simmer for 3 minutes and serve.

Serves: 4.

Chicken Savoy

Recipe Notes
This is a New Jersey tradition that I unlocked the secret to many years ago and is a special dish for a quick, tasty dinner.

12-16	pieces chicken, raw- (2 whole fryers cut in eighths)
1/2	tablespoon pepper
1/2	tablespoon salt
1	tablespoon garlic, fresh minced
1	tablespoon garlic powder
1	teaspoon oregano, dried
1	teaspoon basil, dried
2	cups Parmesan cheese, grated
1/2	cup balsamic vinegar

Instructions

You will need non-stick cooking spray.

Preheat oven to 450°.

Wash and clean chicken pieces. Season with salt and pepper. Mix cheese with spices in plastic bag. Shake pieces of chicken in bag to coat.

Spray 3 quart roasting pan with non-stick spray and put chicken pieces in so they do not touch. Roast for 35 minutes. Pour the balsamic evenly over the chicken. Turn off the oven and return the pan to the oven for 15 minutes to finish cooking.

If cooking boneless fillets... 15 minutes in 450° oven and 10 minutes in turned off oven to finish.

Serves: 6.

Mom's Soupy Chicken

Recipe Notes

You can add fresh or frozen peas or asparagus to make this more colorful and nutritious.

I used to call this "Tennis Court Chicken" because I could spend all day on the court and still have dinner on the table at 6 p.m. Boy, is life different!

2	frying chickens, cut in eighths
1	cup flour
1	teaspoon salt
1/2	teaspoon black pepper, freshly ground
2	teaspoons garlic powder
1	teaspoon paprika
1 1/2	cups onions, chopped
1/4	cup olive oil
2	cans cream of mushroom soup, canned condensed
1	can water

Instructions

Preheat the oven to 350°.

Mix the flour and spices in a plastic bag and shake the chicken parts to coat.

Heat the oil in a large skillet and lightly brown the onions. Add the chicken pieces and brown. Remove pieces as they brown an place in a large oven safe casserole. Add more oil as necessary to brown all the chicken. Mix the soup with the water and pour over the chicken. Cover with foil and bake for 45 minutes.

Serve over rice or noodles.

Serves: 6.

Poached Chicken with Mushroom Sauce

Recipe Notes
If you have a packet sealing system you can use it to enclose the chicken pieces and leave them in the fridge until time to cook.

4	whole chicken breasts, boneless & skinless, halved
2	packages Frozen Chopped Spinach, thawed
1	medium onion, diced
1	tablespoon olive oil
1/4	cup Egg Substitute
4	ounces feta cheese
4	ounces farmer cheese
1/3	cup bread crumbs
1/2	teaspoon salt
1/2	teaspoon black pepper, ground
3	tablespoons unsalted butter
3	tablespoons olive oil
1/2	pound Crimini Mushroom, sliced
1/2	pound button mushroom, sliced
2	scallions, minced
1/4	cup dry sherry
1/2	cup chicken broth
1	teaspoon cornstarch
1/2	cup heavy cream

Instructions

Drain the spinach by squeezing in a towel or pressing in a colander.

Filling:

Brown the onions in oil and then stir in the spinach. Cook over medium heat for 2-3 minutes. Beat eggs with cheeses and stir into spinach. Season with salt and pepper and add bread crumbs slowly to absorb liquids. Cool.

Cut a pocket in the side of each breast half and stuff with about 2 Tbsp. of spinach. Roll each in heavy plastic wrap and twist the ends tight. Chill for 20 minutes.

Bring a large pot of water to a boil, drop in the chicken packets and simmer for 20 minutes.

To make the sauce:

Heat the oil and butter in a large skillet. Add the mushrooms and scallions and cook until wilted by not browned. Stir in the Sherry and cook a few minutes to reduce. Add chicken broth. Mix the cornstarch into the cream until smooth and add to the skillet. Bring to a boil and simmer for two minutes. Keep warm or reheat if made early.

Remove the chicken packets from the water, unwrap and slice on the diagonal. Place the fanned slices on a plate and cover with warmed sauce.

Serves: 6.

Turkey Tetrazzini

Recipe Notes

What is old is new again...with time always a concern, this is a do ahead that uses left overs...doesn't get much easier than that. If you must, make it low fat with substitutions...but it won't be the same.

12	ounces mushrooms, sliced
6	tablespoons unsalted butter
4	tablespoons flour
1 1/2	cups chicken stock
1	cup heavy cream
1	tablespoon dry sherry
1/2	teaspoon salt
1/2	teaspoon black pepper, freshly ground
16	ounces cappellini, cooked al dente and drained
3	cups cooked turkey, cubed
1	cup Parmesan cheese

Instructions

Preheat the oven to 350°.

Melt 2 tbsp. butter in a large skillet and saute the mushrooms until tender and most of the liquid has evaporated.

In a separate large skillet (if you don't have two, do the mushrooms and transfer to a bowl and then use the original skillet to continue) melt the 4 Tbsp. butter and whisk in flour over medium heat. Cook a few minutes, remove from the heat and stir in the broth and cream. Whisk until combined and return to medium heat to cook mixture until it comes to a boil. Add the Sherry and the salt and pepper.

Mix the sauce, cooked pasta and mushrooms. Butter a 3 quart casserole and place half the pasta mixture in bottom. Top this with all of the turkey cubes and distribute evenly. Sprinkle with a 1/2 cup of the parmesan.Top with the rest of the pasta and then the rest of the cheese.

Bake for 30 minutes until brown and bubbling.

Serves: 8.

Meats

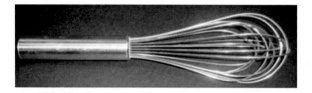

Buy an instant read thermometer to check the internal temperatures of your meat for correct degree of doneness.

Steak au Poivre, p. 101

Sausage, Onions and Peppers, p. 100

Ham Steaks, p. 97

Stuffed Brisket of Beef, p. 103

Chili-The World's Best, 93

Chinese Spareribs, 94

Chili- The World's Best

Recipe Notes

This recipe came to me from my friend, Judy Betteley, back in my Syracuse days.
You can make this hotter with hot chili powder or more cayenne or red pepper flakes....adding chipotle gives the chili a smokiness.
You can place a scoop of rice under the chili, add a salad and corn bread to make a complete meal.
It is always a great addition to a party buffet.
Surround the pot with toppings of: chopped onions, shredded cheddar, black olives, jalapenos and chopped cilantro.

1/2	pound bacon
6	cloves garlic, minced
2	cups onions, chopped
2	pounds lean ground beef
2	28 oz. cans red kidney beans
2	16 oz. cans tomato sauce
2	tablespoons tomato paste
3	tablespoons chili powder
1	teaspoon red pepper flakes, optional
1	tablespoon salt
1	bottle of dark beer

Instructions

Put bacon in freezer for 30 minutes. Set a timer because we both know you will forget it.
When it is solid slice across it to make very small pieces.

Heat a large pot over medium heat. Put bacon, onions and garlic in the pot and cook until the onions are soft. Do not brown.

Add the beef and stir until all the pink is gone and meat is lightly browned. Pour the mixture through a strainer to get rid of the fat. Return the meat to the pot with the beans and their liquid. Add the rest of the ingredients.

Bring to a boil and reduce the heat and simmer, uncovered, for two hours. Add more water if needed. Do not let scorch. As with any "stew like" mixture, you can bake at 325 for two hours. Stir occasionally.

Serves: 8.

Chinese Spareribs

Recipe Notes
Use one pound of ribs per person or more if you know your crowd.
If you want these as an appetizer, count the ribs and allow three per person.

4	pounds pork spareribs, trimmed
3	tablespoons soy sauce
1	teaspoon garlic powder
1	tablespoon dry sherry
3	tablespoons Hoisin Sauce
3	tablespoons chicken broth
6	tablespoons bottled duck sauce

Instructions

Preheat oven to 350°.

Cut ribs into 4 rib racks. Mix soy sauce, garlic powder, dry sherry, Hoisin sauce and chicken broth. Combine mixture with the ribs in a large roasting pan. Stir to coat the ribs.

Make foil packages of three racks (each four ribs) stacked on top of one another and sealed well. Lay the packages on a rimmed cookie sheet (they can be on top of each other.)

Bake for 50 minutes.

Unwrap the ribs and reserve the sauce from the packets. Turn up the oven to 400. Place the ribs on a rack and brush with the reserved sauce. Bake for 15 mintes until glazed. Baste every 5 minutes. Serve with jarred duck sauce.

Serves: 4.

Espresso Crusted Beef Tenderloin

<u>Recipe Notes</u>
This is special enough for a dinner for New Year's Eve.
I once made a whole filet to use the beef for the most wonderful Roast Beef Hash...that was a great brunch!

1	whole beef tenderloin (4-5 lbs.)
1	tablespoon espresso powder
1	tablespoon brown sugar
1	teaspoon salt
1	teaspoon black pepper, freshly ground
1	tablespoon olive oil
1	cup balsamic vinegar
1/2	teaspoon dried thyme
1/4	cup unsalted butter
1	cup beef broth
1/4	teaspoon black pepper, cracked

Instructions

Heat oven to 450°.

Combine the espresso powder, brown sugar, salt and pepper with the olive oil and rub all over the meat.

Place roast in a shallow roasting pan. Roast for 15 minutes and then lower the heat to 350 and roast 30 minutes more. DO NOT OPEN THE DOOR! This will give you rare. Five minutes more will be medium rare...don't even consider well done! Take out and tent with foil and let rest for 15 minutes. Skim the fat from the drippings and reserve.

To make the sauce: Bring the balsamic vinegar and the thyme to a boil in a small nonreactive saucepan...stainless is preferred...cook over medium heat for 20 minutes or until reduced to 1/4 cup. Mix butter and flour in a small bowl until smooth. Add broth, reserved drippings and pepper to saucepan. Gradually whisk in butter mixture until smooth; bring to a boil. Reduce the heat and simmer until thickened. Keep warm and serve over sliced beef.

Serves: 8.

Grilled Butterflied Leg of Lamb

<u>Recipe Notes</u>
An easy meal any time of the year. Lamb that is marinated is great even for people that say they don't like the flavor of plain lamb.

*If you broiling or grilling indoors, be sure to have adequate ventilation.
Be sure to pour off any fat as it accumulates.*

6	pounds leg of lamb, boned and butterflied
3/4	cup olive oil
1/4	cup lemon juice
1	tablespoon red wine vinegar
1	cup onion, diced
1	cup carrot, diced
1	tablespoon garlic, minced
2	bay leaves
1/2	teaspoon dried thyme
1/2	teaspoon dried oregano
1/2	teaspoon black pepper, freshly ground
1 1/2	teaspoons salt

Instructions

Cut as much fat off the lamb as possible.

Combine the marinade ingredients and pour into a roasting pan large enough to hold the lamb flat. Cover and refrigerate overnight.

In the morning, turn over the lamb, recover and refrigerate until ready to cook. Remove from fridge one hour before cooking.

Heat grill or broiler to high. Start the lamb, meaty side down for 15 minutes, turn and cook 10-12 minutes more for pink.

Thinner sections may need to be removed so they are not too well done. Our Greek friends eat their lamb well done so you can have some degree of doneness for one and all.

Serves: 10.

Ham Steaks

<u>Recipe Notes</u>
You don't need a whole ham to have a holiday meal.
If you have time to make the Layered Sweet and White Potato Casserole, you will have a terrific dinner. You could also serve plain baked sweet potatoes and some kind of sauteed greens.

3	pounds ham steaks
1	can 20 ounce, pineapple rings and juice
1/2	cup brown sugar
1	teaspoon dry mustard powder

Instructions

Heat broiler to high.

Cut the steaks in half pound serving pieces.

Drain the juice from the pineapple rings. Mix 1/2 the juice with the sugar and the mustard. Spread on ham steaks and the pineapple rings. Broil about 6 inches from the flame until brown and bubbling.

Serve the steaks with the pineapple on top.

Serves: 6.

Jaden's Meatloaf

Recipe Notes

This is my grandson, Jaden's, favorite Nana meal. It is a frequent request item on Nana's restaurant menu. (Nana's Restaurant is only open for family Sunday dinners.)

*Add 1/2 parmesan cheese to the mixture and shape into meatballs.
Bake at 350 about 45 minutes or until done.*

2	pounds lean ground beef
1	egg, beaten
1/4	cup ketchup
1/4	cup lite soy sauce
1	teaspoon black pepper, freshly ground
1	teaspoon salt
2	slices white bread, crust removed
1/4	cup water

Instructions

Preheat oven to 350°.

Tear bread into small pieces and soak in water.

Put ground meat in large bowl and add the eggs, ketchup, soy, salt and pepper. Add the bread and water and stir well. (I always mix with my hands...but that's me.)

You can spray a 4 X 9 X 4 loaf pan with non stick spray or use four mini loaf pans to make individual portions. Pack the meat into the pan and press down gently. Make a sqiggle of ketchup along the top and bake for 40 minutes. Let rest for 10 minutes and then pour off excess fat from pan.

Serves: 4.

Osso Buco

Recipe Notes
This is a really expensive dinner..for very special guests.
This is a dish that tastes better the second or third day.
Try to make it in advance. You can also make the same recipe with lamb or pork shanks for a completely different dish and much more econonmical. For the lamb, I would add rosemary, for the pork, sage to the cooking liquid.

8	1 1/2 inch thick, slices of veal shank
1/2	cup flour
1	teaspoon salt
1/2	teaspoon black pepper, freshly ground
1/2	cup onion, minced
3	cloves garlic, minced
2	ribs celery, minced
2	carrots, minced
2	tablespoons parsley, chopped
1	28 oz. can peeled tomatoes, crushed
1/4	teaspoon crushed red pepper flakes
1	cup dry white wine
1	cup water
1	chicken bouillon cube

Instructions
Mix the flour with salt and pepper in a plastic bag. Dredge the veal slices by shaking in the bag. Set aside the veal.

Heat the oil in a large heavy pot with a tight fitting lid.

Brown the veal slices on all sides and remove to a platter until all are browned.

In the same pot, saute the onion, garlic,carrots and celery until wilted. Cook over medium heat until all the veggies are soft.

Return the veal to the pot and add the remaining ingredients.

Bring to a boil and reduce the heat and simmer for one hour. Be sure to stir every now and then so it does not stick.   The meat should be tender but not falling off the bone. You could also put this in a 350° oven. If it gets too thick add a little chicken stock or water.

Serves: 4.

Sausage, Onions and Peppers

Recipe Notes

You can use any varity of sausage. Hot or sweet. Pork, beef or poultry. There are so many chicken sausages available and they are already cooked. Just simmer for 5 minutes and then proceed with the recipe.
If using as a topping on pasta, add a jar of marinara sauce to mixture.

2	pounds sausage, hot or sweet Italian
1	cup red wine
4	green peppers, cut in strips
2	large onions, sliced

Instructions

Pierce the sausages several times with a fork and place in a large skillet with one cup of red wine and enough water to cover. Boil for 10 minutes.

Drain the sausages and then brown them in the same skillet.If you are using chicken sausage, as I usually do, you will have to add a little oil to brown them. Remove the sausage and leave or add 2 tablespoons of fat.

Cook the peppers and onions until brown, slice the sausage on the diagonal in one inch slices and add back to the skillet to reheat.

Serves: 8.

Steak au Poivre

<u>Recipe Notes</u>
Very festive done in view of your guests. Watch out when you flame this..stir until flame goes out.
Make the steaks the right size for your guests appetites.

6	individual club steaks, room temperature
2	tablespoons black pepper, cracked
1	tablespoon kosher salt
6	tablespoons unsalted butter
1/2	teaspoon Tabasco sauce
1	teaspoon Worcestershire sauce
1	Juice of one lemon
2	tablespoons cognac
1	tablespoon parsley, chopped
1	tablespoon chives, chopped

Instructions

Sprinkle both sides of the steaks with the cracked pepper and press into the meat with the heel of your hand. Let stand about 30 minutes.

Sprinkle a light layer of Kosher salt in a large skillet that will hold all the steaks. Heat until very hot. Sear steaks for four minutes and then turn, lower heat and cook about three minutes more for very rare. (increase timing in minute increments for more doneness.)

Place a teaspoon of butter on each steak,a few drops of Tabasco, a splash of worcestershire sauce and drizzle of lemon juice. Pour brandy into the skillet, step back and ignite. Swirl the sauce and baste the steaks with it.

Set the steaks on plates or platter and sprinkle with the chopped parsley and chives.

Serves: 6.

Stuffed Brisket of Beef

<u>Recipe Notes</u>
Elegant enough for a holiday dinner. Carrot pudding and Kasha would make a great plate.

2	boxes Stouffer's Spinach Souffle
5	pounds beef brisket
4	tablespoons canola oil
1	tablespoon black pepper, ground
1	tablespoon paprika
2	onions, coarsely chopped
4	carrots, coarsely chopped
3	stalks celery, coarsely chopped
1	cup coffee
1 1/2	cups beef broth
1/2	cup gingersnap, crumbled

Instructions
Defrost the spinach souffle. About 2 hours.
Preheat oven to 325°.

Make a pocket in the side of the beef leaving a one inch border of meat all around the cut. (The butcher can do this for you.)

Push the spinach or any other stuffing into the pocket...be sure to get in all the way in the back. Close the open end with tooth picks and twine. (I use unwaxed dental floss to close the pocket by criss crossing the toothpicks to keep secure.) Push down on top of meat to distribute the stuffing and flatten.
Heat the oil in a large skillet. Season with pepper and paprika on both sides and brown in the oil, turning once. Spray a roasting pan with non-stick spray and put the meat in it. Add the veggies to the skillet and brown lightly. Mix the coffee and the beef broth together and pour into the skillet stirring to pick up the browned bits. Pour the mixture over the meat in the pan. Cover tightly with foil and put in oven for 3 hours.

Remove the meat, let cool then wrap in foil and refrigerate.. Add the cookies to the liquid in the roasting pan and cook over medium heat for about 15 minutes to thicken the sauce. Push the sauce through a coarse sieve. Refrigerate the sauce in a separate container overnight. Defat the sauce when chilled.

Slice the meat against the grain with stuffing in each slice. Put slices in pan with a little sauce, cover with foil and reheat in oven. Serve the extra sauce on the side.

Serves: 6.

White Lamb Stew

<u>Recipe Notes</u>
OK! This is not really as uncomplicated as I usually am....but it is not hard to make.
There are a few extra steps that most recipes don't have but are so worth doing it the correct way.
This is a recipe that was from Gourmet Magazine in 1963.
Really can't do much to improve these results.
TRY IT!
By the way, over the years, I have had left over sauce when the lamb is gone. This has become a soup when mixed with the reserved broth.
Sort of a cream of lamb soup with veggies, or"lamb vichyssoise".

3	large leeks, coarsely chopped
3	pounds lean boneless lamb shoulder or leg, cubed
2	pounds lamb, bone in neck and meat, cubed
4	large onions, coarsely chopped
3	cloves garlic, smashed
1 1/2	tablespoons salt
1/4	teaspoon black pepper
1/4	teaspoon cayenne pepper
2	bay leaves
6	cups water
18	small boiling potatoes
1	box baby onions, frozen
24	baby carrots
1	package petite frozen peas, defrosted
1/4	cup fresh parsley, chopped

Instructions

Put lamb in a 5 quart heavy pot and cover with cold water. Simmer uncovered for 5 minutes. Drain lamb in colander, then rinse with cold water. Wash pot.

Use only the white and pale green parts of the leeks. Wash leeks in a bowl of cold water, then lift out and drain well in a sieve.

Peel and coarsely chop large boiling potatoes, then add to pot with leeks, chopped onions, celery, garlic, salt, pepper and 6 cups of water. Bring to a boil and add lamb, then reduce heat and simmer, uncovered, stirring occasionally, about one hour.

Transfer lamb with tongs to a small bowl.

Transfer solids from the pot with a slotted spoon to a blender until half full. Add about 1 1/2 c. of the broth. Put on lid and cover with a towel. Hold down lid and pulse until smooth.) Be careful using a blender with hot liquids because the heat expands the air and it can pot the top up.) Repeat with all the solids and reserve any broth that is left.

Put lamb back in the sauce and refrigerate over night. Remove any congealed fat from the chilled stew before continuing.

Put the potatoes in a pot of cold water to cover and bring to a boil. Simmer for about 10 minutes until tender when pierced with a fork. Remove from the pot and put in the carrots. Cook until tender, remove and add the onions.

While the veggies are cooking reheat the lamb and sauce in a large pot. Add the veggies as they finish and add the peas to the pot and heat all together about 5 minutes more. Top each portion with chopped parsley when serving.

Serves: 6.

Seafood

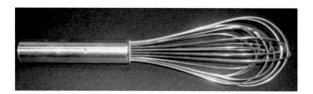

Be sure that your fish is fresh! Use your sense of smell...if the fish has one...it is NOT fresh.

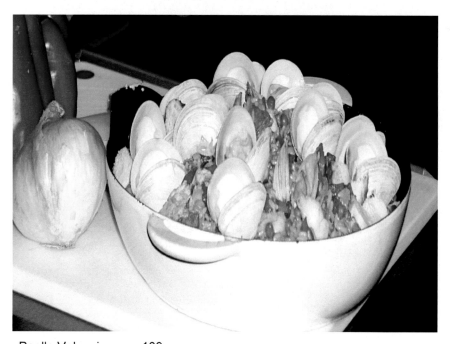

Paella Valenciana, p. 109

Fabulous Fish Fillets, p. 108

Shrimp de Jonghe, p. 113

Shrimp in Green Sauce, p. 114

Clambake Anytime

Recipe Notes
I was making The Barefoot Contessa's Recipe for Kitchen Clambake for a very long time when I thought of a few changes. The original is still a winner but this one is a good variation.
You will need a large lobster pot or16-20 quart pot to make this. It is worth investing in one because you will make this all the time.
Also, be sure to use a good dry white sauvignon blanc or vermouth for the wine.

1/4	cup olive oil
4	leeks, chopped
2	large onions, chopped
2	dozens little neck clams
2	dozens mussels, cleaned
1 1/2	pounds small new potatoes
1	pound kielbasa sausage, sliced
6	corn on cob, halved
1/2	pound shrimp, peeled and cleaned
1	tablespoon salt
2	teaspoons black pepper, freshly ground
2	cups dry white wine
3	small lobsters, optional

Instructions
Heat the oil in a large skillet and saute the onions and the white part of the leeks. Cook until the leeks are wilted and the onions are golden.

Layer the ingredients in the large pot as follows:
The clams, mussels, leeks and onions, potatoes, kielbasa, corn, shrimp and then the lobster cut in pieces if serving eight or in half if serving six. Pour in the wine. Cover the pot tightly and cook over medium-high heat until steam just begins to escape from the lid, about 15-20 minutes without lobster, 40 minutes with lobster. Lower the heat and cook about 15 minutes more.

Serves: 8.

Fabulous Fish Fillets

Recipe Notes
Fast dinner for even the pickiest fish eater!

1/2	pound mushrooms, sliced
3	tablespoons olive oil
2	pounds fish fillets (sole, flounders, etc)
1	teaspoon salt
1/2	teaspoon pepper, freshly ground
1	cup milk
1	tablespoon unsalted butter
1	tablespoon flour
2	tablespoons Parmesan cheese, grated
1/2	cup heavy cream
3	teaspoons jarred pimentos, chopped

Instructions

Preheat oven to 400°.

Heat oil in a large skillet over medium heat and saute the mushrooms about 5 minutes stirring occasionally. Season with salt and pepper. Remove to a bowl and wipe out skillet.

Put milk in the skillet and bring to a simmer over low heat. Add fish and poach 5-10 minutes depending on the thickness of the fillets. Remove the fish to a warm platter.

Mix the butter and flour together with your fingers and stir into the milk. Add the cheese and cream and stir constantly with a whisk until thickened into a medium thick white sauce. Stir in the chopped pimentos.

Put fish into an au gratin dish, top with mushrooms and sauce.

Bake uncovered for 10 minutes.

Serve over rice or orzo mixed with parsley.

Serves: 4.

Paella Valenciana

Recipe Notes
You need a 14 inch skillet or a real Paella pan for this recipe. You might want to share one with a friend. When I first made this 40 years ago, I borrowed a 20 inch cast iron skillet from a neighbor. It sat on all four burners and needed two people to move it.

Boy, has this got a lot of ingredients! But it is a one dish meal with a salad and bread. So get all the items out and measured and you will be rewarded with the best party dish ever. Can stretch to feed 10-12 easily.

2	pounds chicken thighs, boneless
2	tablespoons olive oil
1	tablespoon paprika
2	cloves garlic, minced
1/2	teaspoon black pepper, freshly ground
1	28 oz. can peeled tomatoes, peeled and chopped
2	cups chicken broth
1	teaspoon tumeric
1	a few strands of saffron
1	box artichoke hearts, defrosted
2	cups onions, chopped
1	cup green pepper, diced
1/2	pound pepperoni, thinly sliced
1/2	pound sea scallops, cleaned
1	teaspoon dried oregano
2	teaspoons salt
2	tablespoons olive oil
1 1/2	cups Uncle Ben's Rice, uncooked
1	pound raw shrimp, cleaned
2	cups frozen peas, uncooked
1	pound mussels, cleaned
1	dozen little neck clams, cleaned

Instructions

You could use any cut of chicken on or off the bone cut in one inch pieces. In a gallon baggie combine: 2 Tbsp. olive oil, paprika, garlic, oregano, pepper and salt. Place the chicken in the bag and knead to cover with all the spices. This can marinate overnight or just as long as it takes to prep the rest of the ingredients.

In a large pot combine: tomatoes, chicken broth, turmeric, saffron and artichoke hearts.

Bring to a boil over high heat; turn off the heat. Set aside.

Heat 2 Tbsp. olive oil in a very large skillet (14") and cook the onions and peppers until soft but not brown. Add the pepperoni and cook until hot. Add the chicken and its marinade and stir until chicken loses all the pink color. Add the rice, stir until the rice is coated with the oil in the pan. Add the tomato mixture, cover and cook for about 15 minutes. Uncover, stir well, add the shrimp, scallops, peas and pimientos. Cover and cook for about 15 minutes more until all the liquid is absorbed.

If rice is cooked and there is extra liquid, siphon off some and reserve.
While the rice is cooking, steam the clams and mussels until they open. Discard any that don't open.

Place the clams and mussels on the top of paella attractively. (I cook the clams and mussels separately so that their sand does not go into the paella.)

If you can obtain a small steamed lobster, put it on the top for the presentation.

Sangria for a Crowd

1   cup Peach Brandy
5   Oranges, cut into eights, unpeeled
3   Lemons sliced
2   Limes, sliced
10   ounces peach brandy
1   gallon dry white wine, chilled
2   quarts club soda, chilled

Combine fruit and peach brandy. Let fruit soften in brandy overnight in a glass pitcher or bowl.

Place fruit and brandy in a punch bowl and add wine and soda. Float ice mold in bowl to keep it cold.

To Make Ice Mold:
Take a bundt pan or any ring mold. Cut up and arrange a layer of fresh fruit (lemon or lime slices,grapes, cherries) in bottom of mold. Pour 1" of bottled water over fruit and freeze. Continue to layer fruit and water, freezing each layer before adding the next. To unmold, dip briefly in hot water or wrap in hot towel.

Serves: 8.

Shibui Scallops

Recipe Notes

An elegant appetizer at the table. Last minute preparation is important so I would not make this for a crowd. It would impress the in-laws for a first meet and greet.
You can find the red salmon caviar in the grocery store at the deli or in the fish section. There are many domestic caviars that are great...one is wasabi that is bright green .
You can buy seaweed salad at Asian groceries or maybe your local Japanese restaurant will sell you some.
Special note: *Buy only dry scallops...they will brown. Ask the fish monger if they are wet or dry....dry is all you want! Wet scallops are treated and will always exude liquid and not brown well.*

1	tablespoon wasabi powder
1	tablespoon water
1/4	cup sour cream
12	large sea scallops, rinsed and drained
1/2	cup flour
1/2	teaspoon salt
1/2	teaspoon black pepper, freshly ground
1	egg
2	egg whites
1	cup panko bread crumbs
1	teaspoon Crab boil, Bay seasoning or anyother seafood spice
2	tablespoons butter
2	tablespoons canola oil
1	jar Red salmon caviar

Instructions
To make the Shibui sauce: stir the water into the wasabi powder until smooth and then stir in the sour cream. Set aside.

Lightly toss the scallops in the flour. Roll each scallop in egg and then in crumbs and set aside until all are coated. Refrigerate for 1/2 hour.

Heat a large skillet over medium heat. When hot, add oil and butter. When the butter is foaming, add the scallops to the pan and cook until browned underneath about three minutes (do not move the scallops for two minutes to set up the browned side) and then turn to brown other side. Remove to paper towel to drain.

Place one or two scallops in a scallop shell and then about a 1 1/2 tsp. of the sauce on the top. Spoon on a teaspoon of the caviar and surround with seaweed salad.
Serves: 6.

Shrimp Creole

<u>Recipe Notes</u>
Another from the freezer when there is nothing to eat...

2	tablespoons unsalted butter
2	tablespoons olive oil
1/2	cup onion, finely chopped
1	large green pepper, chopped
1/2	tablespoon red pepper flakes, optional
1	teaspoon salt
1/2	teaspoon pepper, ground
1 1/2	pounds frozen cooked cocktail shrimp, defrosted
2	cups jarred marinara sauce

Instructions

Heat butter or oil in a large skillet.

Saute the onion and pepper until wilted but not brown, about 10 minutes on medium heat; add red pepper flakes. Cut the shrimp in half and add to the onion with marinara sauce and heat through. Season with salt and pepper to taste.

Serve with rice.

Serves: 6.

Shrimp de Jonghe

<u>Recipe Notes</u>
A wonderful casserole for a buffet. Easy to prepare and very tasty.

2	pounds Shrimp (cleaned), 16-20 count
1 1/2	cups Panko Bread Crumbs
10	tablespoons unsalted butter, melted
1/4	cup scallions, chopped
2	cloves garlic, minced
2	tablespoons parsley, chopped
1	teaspoon fresh tarragon
1	teaspoon vinegar
1	teaspoon thyme
1/2	cup sherry
1	teaspoon salt
1/2	tablespoon pepper, freshly ground

Instructions

Preheat oven to 350°.

Wash the shrimp and dry well. Combine one cup of the Panko crumbs with the 8 tablespoons of butter, scallions, garlic, parsley, vinegar, thyme, sherry, salt and pepper.

Butter a 1 1/2 quart casserole and layer the shrimp and bread crumbs, starting and ending with the shrimp. Combine the remaining butter and bread crumbs and sprinkle over the top.   Bake for one hour until nicley browned.

Serves: 6.

Shrimp in Green Sauce

Recipe Notes
This could be used with scallops or clams or a mixture of all.

2	tablespoons olive oil
3	tablespoons scallions, chopped including greens
3	cloves garlic, fresh minced, minced
1 1/2	tablespoons flour
1/4	cup white wine
2/3	cup clam juice
2	tablespoons milk
1	cup fresh parsley, minced
1/4	teaspoon cayenne pepper
1	teaspoon freshly ground black pepper
1 1/2	pounds Shrimp (cleaned), 16-20 count

Instructions

Heat oil over medium heat in a non-stick fry pan. Saute scallions until wilted but not brown. Add garlic and stir for one minute more. Stir in the flour and cook for a few minutes, stirring constantly.

Mix together white wine, clam juice and milk, stir into skillet gradually. Add parsley, cayenne and pepper. Cook stirring constantly until smooth and thick. Add shrimp, cover and simmer until shrimp are pink and cooked, approximately 5-6 minutes.

Serve with rice or orzo.

Serves: 4.

Shrimp Scampi

Recipe Notes
There is no such thing as too much garlic.

2	pounds shrimp, raw, deveined and peeled
4	tablespoons unsalted butter
4	tablespoons olive oil
4	tablespoons minced garlic
1/2	teaspoon crushed red pepper
1	teaspoon salt
2	tablespoons lemon juice
3	tablespoons parsley, chopped

Instructions

Melt butter and oil in a large skillet over medium heat until bubbling. Add the garlic and saute until golden-DO NOT BURN! Add crushed red pepper, salt and half the parsley. Add the shrimp and stir until they turn pink.

Sprinkle with lemon juice and remaining parsley.

Serve over rice or orzo pasta.

Serves: 6.

Vegetables

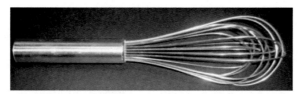

If you can increase your number of vegetables and fresh fruits, your daily diet improves dramatically. Make a few of the following recipes and skip the protein one day a week.

Harvest Tomato Casserole, p. 122

Carrot-Parsip Latkes, p. 120

Spicy Corn Pudding, p. 126

Roasted Asparagus, p. 125

Carmelized Onions and Chestnuts

Recipe Notes
Winter dish that is rich and sweet.

2	pound cippolini onions (or any small onions)
1	14-16 oz.jar chestnuts, roasted
4	tablespoons unsalted butter
1	pinch salt
1	pinch pepper
4	tablespoons dark brown sugar
1	cup chicken stock

Instructions

Peel the onions. Bring a pot of salted water to a boil and blanch the onions for four minutes. Drain and put on cookie sheet to cool.

Heat a large skillet over medium heat, melt the butter and add the onions. Roll them to coat with butter and then add the chestnuts. Season with salt and pepper and sprinkle with brown sugar. Cook until the sugar caramelizes, about 3-4 minutes, then add the broth. Cook over low heat, until the liquid is reduced to a syrupy texture, 15-20 minutes.

This goes along side any piece of meat or game dish.

Serves: 8.

Carrot and Parsnip Latkes

Recipe Notes

These are good as a side dish, too.

As good as potato pancakes are, these are good, too.
Different but really good! Pretty colors help the presentation for a plate of white food...like a fish supper.

1	large Idaho potato, peeled and grated
2	medium carrots, peeled and grated
2	medium parsnips, peeled and grated
1/4	cup matzoh cracker
2	large eggs, beaten
2	tablespoons onions, chopped
1	tablespoon parsley, chopped
1	tablespoon salt
1	pinch freshly ground black pepper
1/2	cup canola oil

Instructions

Toss potato, carrots and parsnips with matzoh meal. Add the eggs, onion, parsley, salt and pepper. Mix well.

Heat ¼ inch canola oil in skillet. Drop batter by tablespoons into oil....brown on one side, about 5 minutes, turn and brown other side.

Drain on absorbent toweling and salt lightly with sea salt.

Serves: 6.

Carrot Pudding

Recipe Notes
Great with Stuffed Brisket! Not a Passover dish but good any other time of the year.

1	cup Matzoh Meal
1	teaspoon salt
1	teaspoon cream of tartar
1	teaspoon baking soda
3/4	cup vegetable shortening
1/2	cup brown sugar
3	eggs, separated
3	cups carrots, grated

Instructions

Preheat oven to 350°.

Sift together the dry ingredients. Cream sugar and shortening. Beat egg yolks until light. Alternately add egg yolks and dry ingredients to the creamed mixture, mix well. Stir in the carrots. Beat egg whites until stiff and gently fold into mixuture. Bake in a well-greased mold or a 9 x 4 loaf pan.

Bake for 40 minutes. Test in center with a long toothpick. If it is wet, bake another 10 minutes and test again.

Serve hot or cold as a vegetable.

Serves: 8.

Harvest Tomato Casserole

Recipe Notes
In the fall, there are Heirloom tomatoes of all colors.
Mix as many as you can find in this beautiful dish.

1	pound red tomato
1	pound yellow tomato
1	pint grape tomato
1	28 oz. can peeled tomatoes, diced
2	tablespoons olive oil
1/2	cup onion
2	tablespoons garlic, minced
6	sprigs fresh thyme
1	tablespoon fresh thyme, leaves
1	cup Panko Bread Crumbs
1/2	cup Parmesan cheese, grated

Instructions

Bring a large pot of water to a boil and blanch red and yellow tomatoes for 30 seconds. Remove them to a bowl of cold water to stop the cooking. Slip off their skins, cut in half horizontally and squeeze out the seeds. Cut each piece in half again and set aside.

Preheat oven to 400°.

Spray a 2 quart oven proof baking dish with non stick spray.

Heat 2 Tbsp of the olive oil in a large skillet and sauté the minced onion and garlic until soft but not brown. Add all the tomatoes, thyme sprigs and leaves. Stir in 1 Tbsp salt and lots of freshly ground pepper. Turn into prepared baking dish .

Combine crumbs and cheese and sprinkle evenly over the top. Spray top lightly with Non-Stick Cooking Spray. Bake for 10-12 minutes, until browned.

Serves: 6.

Layered Sweet and White Potato Casserole

Recipe Notes
To be the colorful starch on a plate of white food like chicken breasts or fish fillets.

4	sweet potatoes, peeled
4	white potatoes, peeled
3 1/2	cups heavy cream
3/4	cup maple syrup
1/4	cup brown sugar
1/2	teaspoon cinnamon
1	teaspoon salt
1	teaspoon pepper, freshly ground
1/4	pound unsalted butter, cut in pieces

Instructions

Preheat oven to 350°.

Thinly slice potatoes on mandoline or with sharp knife. Butter a 9x13 casserole. Make alternated layers of the sweet and white potatoes. Season with salt and pepper. Press down to compact.

In a sauce pan, bring the cream to a boil with other ingredients and pour over the potatoes. Dot the top with butter pieces.

Spray a piece of foil with non-stick spray. Cover the casserole with the foil and bake for 30 minutes. Uncover and bake 1/2 hour more. Let rest before cutting.

Serves: 6.

Ratatouille Royale

Recipe Notes

This dish is equally good served hot or cold. It makes a marvelous appetizer as well as a side dish. It can be used as a filling for omelettes or crepes.

If you like it spicy, add some crushed red pepper with the onions and garlic.

2	large onions
3	cloves garlic, minced
1/3	cup olive oil
2	large green peppers, cut in strips
2	small eggplant, cubed
4	small zucchini, sliced
2	cups celery, thinly sliced
3	tomatoes, peeled and diced
2	teaspoons salt
1	teaspoon dried basil
1/2	teaspoon black pepper, freshly ground

Instructions

Heat oil in a large skillet over medium heat. Saute the onions and garlic until wilted. Add the zucchini, eggplant, celery and green pepper.Saute about 5 minutes and then add the rest of the ingredients. Cover and cook for about 15-20 minutes.

Remove the cover and cook until vegetables are tender and the juices are thickened.

Serves: 8.

Roasted Asparagus

Recipe Notes
This technique is great for all veggies.

Some of the denser ones like beets and fennel can be blanched in boiling water for one minute and then chilled to stop the cooking.

Proceed with the vegetables after blanching as you do with the asparagus.

2	pounds asparagus
2	tablespoons olive oil
1	teaspoon black pepper, freshly ground
1	teaspoon Sea Salt, freshly ground
1/4	cup Parmesan cheese, grated

Instructions

Preheat oven to 450°.

Trim the asparagus ends and break off where it naturally snaps. If the stems are woody, use a peeler to remove them.

Toss the spears with the olive oil and place on a rimmed cookie sheet.

Season with salt and pepper.

Place in preheated oven and roast for 10 minutes. Stir to turn over the asparagus and roast for 10 minutes more. Be sure to check on them every five minutes to make sure that they are not browning too much. Top with cheese and return to oven for 5 more minutes.

Serves: 6.

Spicy Corn Pudding

Recipe Notes
Everyone loves corn and it is an easy side dish that can be used as part of dinner or on a buffet. Leave out the jalapeno if you are sensitive to the hot stuff.

6	tablespoons unsalted butter
1	jalapeno pepper, minced
1	small onion, minced
1	16 oz. can Creamed Corn
1	16 oz. can Whole Kernel Corn with liquid
1	cup sour cream
16	ounces corn muffin mix

Instructions

Spray a 9 X 13 inch pan with cooking spray.

Heat oven to 350°.

Heat a small skillet and melt butter.

Saute the jalapeno and onion until wilted. Let cool.

In a large bowl mix together all the ingredients including the cooled pepper and onion mix, until just blended. DO NOT OVER MIX!

Pour into prepared pan and bake about 50 minutes until set and lightly browned. Test with toothpick in center to see if ready. If toothpick comes out wet, cook 5 minutes more and test again.

.

Serves: 6.

Spicy Corn Pudding. Low Fat

Recipe Notes
*You can add minced fresh jalapeno pepper to make it a little spicy
be sure to remove the seeds and white fiber inside the peppers to control the heat. And
wash your hands well when you are done. Leave it out if you don't like the heat.*

1	16 oz. can Creamed Corn
1	16 oz. can Whole Kernel Corn with liquid
1	cup Reduced Fat Sour Cream
1/2	cup Egg Substitute
6	tablespoons Smart Balance Spread, melted
1	jalapeno pepper, minced
16	ounces corn muffin mix

Instructions

Spray a 13" x 9" x 2" pan with cooking spray.

Preheat oven to 350°.

Mix all ingredients until just blended and pour into prepared baking dish. Bake uncovered for 50 minutes to 1 hour or until set and lightly browned.

Serves: 6.

Spicy String Beans

<u>Recipe Notes</u>
These are Asian beans and are good as a side dish or as a lunch with rice.
It would be good to do an Asian ingredient shop once in a while in a specialty store.

The Asian sesame oil is toasted and fragrant.

Chili paste with garlic comes in a bottle and is very spicy. Be sure to use with discretion. Fresh ginger is not interchangeable with ground. You can store it in the freezer and use as needed. (If you let sit out and dry it will sprout and make a fabulous plant if you put it in a pot.)

While you are at the Asian market get: Hoisin Sauce, Chinese sausages, soy sauce, rice wine vinegar, dumplings and all kinds of rice.

1	pound string beans
1/2	pound pork shoulder, ground
1	teaspoon chili-garlic sauce
1/2	teaspoon ginger root, minced
1	teaspoon sugar
2	teaspoons dry sherry
1/4	teaspoon salt
2	tablespoons soy sauce, low-salt
1	teaspoon sesame oil

Instructions

It is the chili-garlic paste that makes this spicy. Use sparingly if you are not into the heat. Reduce to 1/4 tsp. so you will still have some of the flavor.

Clean the string beans and remove the tips and tails. Steam about 5 minutes until crisp tender. Drain and rinse under cold water to stop the cooking. Drain again and set aside.

Heat oil in a large skillet until very hot.

Mix together the pork, chili-paste and ginger. Stir fry the pork until is loses it pink color about 3 minutes then add the sugar, sherry and salt. Stir for another minute and then add the soy and sesame oil. Add string beans and stir until heated though.

Serves: 6.

Vegetable Puree

Recipe Notes
You can use this one instead of "Plain Old Mashed Potatoes."

You can use any greens, or root veggie like: carrots, parsnips or celery root mixed with the potato to make this wonderful puree.
If you like, you can add a little cayenne to give it some zip.

4	ounces cream cheese
1	pound russet potato, peeled and cut in cubes
1	pound broccoli
1/2	cup chicken broth, boiling
1/4	cup Parmesan cheese, grated
1	teaspoon salt
1/2	teaspoon black pepper, ground

Instructions

Bring the cream cheese to room temperature.

Place potatoes in a large pot and cover with cold water. Bring to a boil and simmer until tender. About 10 minutes. Drain.

Cook greens in salted water until tender, drain well and then puree in the food processor.

Place potatoes in a large bowl and mash smooth. Add the pureed greens, boiling broth, cream cheese and Parmesan. Whisk well to combine. Season with salt and pepper.

Serves: 8.

Cookies

The best end to any meal is a selection of cookies. Make them small so that people can try several types. More varieties are better than fewer.

Chocolate Chip Cookies, p. 133

Potato Chip Cookies, p. 137

Rugelach-Arlyn's Legacy, p. 139

Rebecca's Chocolate Bars, p. 138

Lacy Cookies, p. 135

Chocolate Chip Cookies- as you remember them

<u>Recipe Notes</u>
These are either soft or crisp... the baking time is the trick...longer is crisper. These are the best...the ones with Crisco. Olivia Burten was the queen of chocolate chips.

3/4	cup Butter Flavored Crisco
1 1/4	cups brown sugar, firmly packed
2	tablespoons milk
1	teaspoon vanilla
1	egg
1 3/4	cups all-purpose flour
1	teaspoon salt
3/4	teaspoon baking soda
1	cup pecans, coarsely chopped
1	cup chocolate chips

Instructions

Preheat oven to 375°.

In the large bowl of the mixer, with the paddle blade, cream the Crisco, brown sugar, milk and vanilla until light and creamy. Blend in the egg.

In a medium sized bowl, sift the flour, salt and baking soda. Stir into creamed mixture in three additions. Stir in nuts and chocolate chips. Measure with 1 tablespoon scoop and place on greased cookie sheet 2 inches apart.

Bake 10- 12 minutes until lightly browned.

Makes: 48.

Cloud Nine Cookies

Recipe Notes

Save the yolks for the Mocha Mousse recipe.

Don't try these on a rainy day...but when you do them, you will be rewarded!

4	egg whites, room temperature
1	pinch salt
1 1/3	cups sugar
1	teaspoon vanilla
1	cup chocolate chips
1	cup coconut, flaked

Instructions

Preheat oven to 300°.

Add the salt to the egg whites and beat to stiff peaks. Add the sugar one tablespoon at a time and continue to beat until stiff and glossy. Add the vanilla half-way throuugh the beating. Fold in the chocolate chips and coconut.

Prepare cookie sheets with ungreased parchment paper and drop the batter by tablespoonsful about two inches apart.

Bake until lightly browned, approx. 25 minutes. Cool slightly and remove to racks to cool completely.

Store in air tight containers.

Makes: 36.

Lace Cookies

Recipe Notes

This recipe makes alot of wonderful cookies. They are great sandwiched with any flavor jam or dark chocolate.

1/4	cup dark corn syrup
1/4	cup molasses
1/2	cup sugar
1	stick unsalted butter
1	cup flour
1/4	teaspoon baking powder
1/2	teaspoon baking soda
1/3	cup pecan, chopped fine

Instructions

Preheat oven to 350°.

Place the corn syrup, molasses, sugar and butter in a one quart pot. Bring to a boil and boil for one minute. Stir in the flour, baking powder, baking soda and nuts. Stir well until completely combined.

Keep over simmering water.

Drop by no more than 1/2 teaspoons, three inches apart on a greased cookie sheet. These really spread!!!! No more than a **half** teaspoon, three inches apart.

Bake 8-10 minutes in preheated oven. Let cool for 2 minutes and remove to a rack to finish cooling.

Makes: 60.

Peanut Butter Balls

Recipe Notes
Beware... these are addictive...serve with napkins on a hot day.

These are Helen Fadini's cookies from thirty years ago...still a peanut fancier's dream.

1/2	pound unsalted butter
16	ounces peanut butter
1	pound Confectioners Sugar
6	ounces dark chocolate
6	ounces milk chocolate

Instructions

In a large bowl of the mixer with the paddle blade, combine the peanut butter and the butter until well blended. Add the sugar and beat on low until entirely incorporated. Chill the mixture for one hour (minimum). Shape to 1/2 inch teaspoon balls. Place balls on waxed paper lined cookie sheets. Place in freezer for a minimum of one hour.

To complete:
Place chocolate in large glass bowl and put in microwave for 20 seconds. Stir very well and repeat at 10 second intervals until melted and smooth. Stir well to increase the shine of the chocolate.

Remove the trays from the freezer one at a time and dip the balls into the chocolate with a toothpick. Slide off onto another waxed paper cookie sheet. You may need extra chocolate. Freeze until ready needed and serve directly from the freezer.

Makes: 60.

Potato Chip Cookies

Recipe Notes
Don't laugh...they really are good and my stint as spokesperson for Pringles financed my teaching kitchen.

You could substitute any nut or extract to change it to what you have in the house. They all work...how about coconut and almond extract.

1	cup unsalted butter, softened
1	cup sugar
1	teaspoon vanilla
1/2	cup pecan, chopped
1/2	heaping cup potato chip, crumbled
2	cups all-purpose flour

Instructions

Preheat oven to 350°.

In the bowl of the mixer, cream the butter and sugar until fluffy. Add the vanilla and flour. Mix again.

Stir in the nuts and potato chips.

Form into small balls and place on ungreased cookie sheet.

Bake for 16-18 minutes or until lightly browned.

Makes: 36.

Rebecca's Best Ever Chocolate Bars

Recipe Notes
You can try a lot of recipes but these bars are as chocolately as they get! Thanks to Carol Smith's, sister in law, Rebecca Kaplan, for weeding out all the others and settling on these.

1/2	cup butter
1/2	cup brown sugar
1	cup flour
2	eggs, beaten
1/2	teaspoon salt
3	tablespoons cocoa
1/2	teaspoon vanilla
2	tablespoons flour
1/2	cup sugar
1/2	cup nut pieces (variety of your choice), chopped

Instructions

Preheat oven to 350°.

Mix together the butter, brown sugar and one cup of flour and press into a 8 x 8 pan to form the bottom crust.

Mix together the rest of the ingredients and pour over the crust. Bake for 35 minutes.

Frost with chocolate frosting or dust with powdered sugar. Cut into small bars.

Makes: 24.

Rugelach-Arlyn's Legacy

Recipe Notes
Arlyn Blake published these "ruggies" about 35 years ago. They are still the best I've ever tasted!

Truth be told, I have a prenatal fear of yeast. If I can do these, you can, too. These are better than any you can buy. Because these are yeast risen, they are lighter than the ususal ones.

1/2	cup sugar
1	teaspoon cinnamon
12	ounces pecans
1	package dry yeast
1/2	cup water, warm
1/2	teaspoon sugar
3	egg yolks
3/4	cup half & half
1	tsp. vanilla extract
1/2	pound unsalted butter
3	cups unbleached flour
1/4	cup sugar
2	cups good jam (any flavor)
1	cup chocolate chips
1	cup raisins, optional
3	egg whites

Instructions

Mix the 1 teaspoon cinnamon with the 1/2 cup of sugar and set aside.

Toast the nuts, chop and set aside, in a bowl or pie dish. To toast nuts: Preheat oven (ore use a toaster oven) to 400°. Spread the nuts on a tray and toast until lightly browned. Watch like a hawk as they tend to burn easily from the oil that is in the nuts.

Dissolve yeast in water with 1/2 tsp. sugar. (If there is no action in the yeast, discard, and start over) Mix egg yolks with half and half in food processor fitted with the steel blade. Add flour, yeast, butter (cut into pieces) vanilla, and 1/4 cup sugar. Pulse on and off until dough forms- run about 10 seconds to knead. Turn onto well floured board. Pat with floured hands into a round. Divide the dough into four smaller round flat disks.

Wrap each disk in waxed paper and refrigerate at least 12 hours or up to 4 days.

Preheat oven to 350 degrees.

When ready to bake, put all your toppings in small bowls. Lightly beat 3 egg whites and have them in a bowl large enought to hold the individual "ruggies."

Remove a disk from the fridge and on a very well -floured board, roll with a well-floured rolling pin into a 10 inch circle. Spread the jam over the dough almost to the very edge. Sprinkle lightly with the reserved cinnamon sugar. Sprinkle on chips and raisins.

With a pizza cutter, cut across the circle from side to side to make 12-16 triangles. Roll each triangle from the outside toward the center into a crescent shape. Dip each crescent into egg whites and the roll in the nuts. Set on prepared pan about 2 inches apart. Repeat with other disks.   Let rise 30 minutes. Bake for 20-25 minutes until golden. Cool on racks.

Makes: 48.

Desserts

Get the desserts made first and out of the way. It takes the pressure off entertaining to have things that can be done in advance finished first.

Pashka, p.156

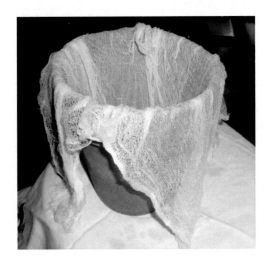

Pashka, p. 156

Chocolate Bark, p. 148

Lovely Lemon Mousse, p. 153

Ambrosia

Recipe Notes
This is a fifties favorite....yes, it is sweet but so what.
It is gooey and sweet and the perfect answer to a mild recession or even a depression.

1	pint sour cream
1	cup pineapple in light syrup, cut in chunks
1	cup mandarin orange sections
1	cup coconut, shredded
3	cups mini marshmallows
1/2	cup walnuts, toasted

Instructions

Drain the fruit and combine all the ingredients except the nuts in a large bowl. Cover and refrigerate overnight.

Serve in a large glass bowl.

Garnish with toasted chopped nuts.

Serves: 8.

Apple Pie

Recipe Notes

For years, I made scratch pie crust but there is no need. Use the rolled pie crust in the box in the refrigerator section of the market. Remove from the refrigerator 20 minutes before baking the pie.

You will not have the" I can't bake pie crust" excuse for not baking pies, ever again.

1	box pie crust, prepared
6	granny smith apples
2/3	cup sugar
2	tablespoons flour
1	teaspoon cinnamon
1	Juice of one lemon
2	tablespoons butter

Instructions

Preheat oven to 425°.

Prepare a bowl of water with the juice of one lemon.

Peel and slice the apples and put into the lemon water as you slice. This will stop the apples from turning brown.

Combine the sugar, flour and cinnamon in a small bowl. Drain the apples and pat to dry a little. Combine with the sugar mixture and set aside about 10 minutes for the apples to give off their juices.

Put one crust in a 9" pie dish. Heap the apples onto the crust and push to the sides and flatten with a spatula. Top with butter cut into small pieces. Wet the rim of the crust with a little water on a brush.

Cut some air slits in other crust and place over the pie. Press the upper crust into the lower using a fork. Trim excess from the edge. Brush the top of the crust with a little milk and sprinkle on a little granulated sugar. Bake 20 minutes and then cover the edge of the pie with aluminum foil to prevent burning. Bake another 30-35 minutes more until pie is bubbling and brown.

Serves: 8.

Carrot Cupcakes

Recipe Notes
Mix a container of whipped cream cheese with 2 Tbsp. of confectioners sugar and spread on top. Add a sprinkle of chopped nuts to the top for a not too sweet dessert.

1 1/2	cups flour, sifted
1	teaspoon baking powder
1	teaspoon baking soda
1	teaspoon cinnamon
1/2	teaspoon salt
1	cup sugar
3/4	cup canola oil
2	eggs
1	cup carrot, grated
1/2	cup walnuts, toasted and chopped

Instructions

Preheat oven to 350°.

Sift flour, baking powder, baking soda, cinnamon and salt in a small bowl.

Combine sugar and oil in a medium bowl and beat thoroughly. Add eggs one at a time, beating after each addition. Mix in carrots. Add dry ingredients gradually, beating until blended. Mix in nuts.

Place cupcake papers in muffin tins. (If you do not have cupcake papers, grease the muffin tins.) Fill cupcake papers ¾'s full. Bake 15-20 minutes. Let cool before frosting.

Makes 12.

Chafing Dish Fruit

Recipe Notes

My friend, Viti Adler, would use this for all her buffet parties.
For the fruit use a mixture of canned and fresh. Adding berries, grapes of all colors and fresh cherries can enhance canned peaches, mandarin oranges, pineapple etc.

Serve hot fruit with a pitcher of the sauce and a bowl of whipped cream along side of the dish for guests to help themselves.

3	egg yolks
1/2	cup sugar
1	cup milk
2	cups heavy cream
1/2	cup confectioners sugar
1/4	cup Grand Marnier Liquor
6	cups Mixed fresh and canned fruit, drained
1/2	cup Kirsch
1/4	cup Kirsch

Instructions

Place the cream, beater and bowl in fridge until needed.

Mix the sugar and yolks in mixer bowl until color is almost white. Bring milk just to a boil. Stir in about 1/4 cup of the milk to the egg yolks beating vigorously so they don't set and then stir into the rest of the milk. Cook over medium heat until just below the boiling point and allow to cool while preparing the cream. Refrigerate the sauce until serving time.

Whip the cream with confectioners' sugar and add the Grand Marnier. Chill in fridge until very cold.

To serve:

Heat the fruit in electric skillet or chafing dish. Add the 1/2 C. Kirsch and continue to heat until the alcohol dissipates. Just before serving you can flame with the other 1/4 C. Kirsch for the big "Da-Da" factor. (Be sure to use long matches and lean back for the big boom.)

Serves: 8.

Cheesecake-the one and only

Recipe Notes
To do this right, you need a standing mixer or great upper arm strength.
This is so good that it is worth the time and the calories. Do not bother to reduce the fat. Just eat nothing else for the week.
I had to eat 110 pieces of cheesecake in judging a contest to find this one! If you ever make one cheesecake this is it.
Leave enough time for it to age before serving.
You can substitute any flavor liqueur for the Grand Marnier. I have used Frangelica, Kahlua and Framboise.
Decorate the top with something that mirrors the flavor you have used. With Grand Marnier I use candied orange slices; Frangelica, I use toasted almonds, Kahlua, chocolate coffee beans etc.

6	eggs, room temperature
1 3/4	cups sugar
1/2	cup all-purpose flour, sifted
32	ounces cream cheese, room temperature
1 1/2	pints sour cream
1 1/2	cups heavy cream
1/3	cup Grand Marnier Liqueur

Instructions

Preheat oven to 350°.

Prepare a 9 inch spring form by buttering and flouring it. Tap out excess flour and set aside.

In a large bowl of the mixer, combine the eggs, sugar and flour, add the cream cheese and blend well. Add the sour cream, Grand Marnier, and heavy cream, beating well after each addition. Total beating time can be 15 minutes.

Pour the mixture into the prepared pan. Place a roasting pan of water on the oven floor and the cake on a shelf directly above it. Bake for 40 minutes and then turn the temperature down to 250 degrees and bake for 50 minutes more. Turn off the oven and leave the door open. Let cool for 4 hours in the oven. Refrigerate for two days before cutting.

Serves: 10.

Chocolate Bark-- The Best Medicine Around

Recipe Notes

Use very good chocolate for this recipe.

Homemade candy is only as good as the ingredients you use...use the best, so you don't waste your time.

I like dark chocolate that is at least 70% cacao- like Scharffen-Berger.
A great holiday variation is to layer the milk chocolate with white chocolate and sprinkle with crushed candy canes before it is set.

1	pound dark, milk or white chocolate
1	cup nut pieces (variety of your choice), toasted and chopped
1	cup fruit (dark red in color ie:dried cranberries, cherries or raisins), dried

Instructions

Break chocolate into small pieces and put in microwave safe glass bowl.

Microwave on high for two minutes, stir, and if not melted, put in for 20 second intervals stirring each time until melted.

Stir in nuts and fruit and pour onto waxed paper lined rimmed cookie sheet.

Use offset spatula and spread evenly to thickness of 1/4".

Put in fridge to harden and then break into small pieces to serve.

Serves: 8.

Chocolate Mousse Pie

Recipe Notes
I have always used homemade chocolate leaves to decorate the top but any pretty chocolate candy could be used on each rosette.

1 1/2	boxes Nabisco Chocolate Wafers
1	stick unsalted butter, melted
16	ounces semisweet chocolate
4	eggs, separated
2	whole eggs
1	teaspoon vanilla
1	cup Confectioners Sugar
4	cups heavy cream

Instructions
Crust: Crush wafers(1/3 box at a time) until fine with a rolling pin or in the food processor. Be sure all lumps are gone.
Mix the crumbs with melted butter and press on the bottom and up the side of a 10 inch spring form pan. Set in the refrigerator for one half hour to set.

Filling: Chop the chocolate into small pieces and put into a glass bowl. Melt in microwave at 2 minute intervals, stirring frequently. Let chocolate cool for ten minutes. Beat in the egg yolks one at a time, then beat in the 2 whole eggs. Make sure to beat well after each egg. Stir in the vanilla.
In the large bowl of the mixer, beat the egg whites(room temperature) until soft peaks form. Add 1/2 cup confectioners sugar, slowly, until the mixture is stiff and not dry.
In another bowl beat 2 cups of heavy cream until firm but not stiff. Fold the whipped cream and egg white mixture alternately into the chocolate mixture. Pour into prepared crust. Chill for 3 hours.

Remove side of springform.

Topping: Beat together 2 cups heavy cream and 1/2 cup sugar until very stiff. Spread a thin layer over the moose and then put the rest into a pastry bag* fitted with a ridged tip. Pipe in a scallop around the edge. Make rosettes in the the center and around the edge. Grate some chocolate on top with a fine grater.

*You can make a pastry bag by filling a gallon plastic bag with the whipped cream and sqeeze into one corner. Twist the top closed and cut off a 1/2 inch piece of the corner. This will allow you to pipe the cream although it won't be as pretty as it is with a decorative tip. When all else fails, there is the canned <u>real</u> whipped cream.

Serves: 12.

Coffee Liqueur Sauce

<u>Recipe Notes</u>
This is great on pound cake or ice cream and especially with the Mocha Mousse.

1 1/2	cups coffee
1 1/2	teaspoons espresso powder
3	tablespoons water
1	tablespoon cornstarch
3/4	cup sugar
2	ounces coffee liqueur

Instructions

Make coffee with 1 1/2 cups of boiling water mixed with the instant espresso powder.

Dissolve the cornstarch in water in small bowl. In a small pot, combine the coffee and sugar and heat until the sugar is dissolved.

Stir the cornstarch and then stir into the coffee. Stir until thickened; cook one minute.

Pour through a strainer into a small pitcher.

Serves: 8.

Flourless Chocolate Cake

Recipe Notes
The cake that everyone will find room for even if they say they are stuffed.

If you place a paper doily on the cake before sifting the sugar on top, it will leave a decorative pattern.

8	ounces dark chocolate
4	ounces semisweet chocolate
1 1/4	cups sugar
8	eggs
12	ounces unsalted butter
1/4	teaspoon salt
1/8	cup Confectioners Sugar

Instructions

Preheat oven 325°.

Prepare a 9 inch spring form pan by buttering well.

Break the chocolate in small pieces and place in a microwave safe glass bowl. Add the butter and salt and microwave on 80% power for 1 1/2 minutes. Stir and microwave again for about a minute and check to see if completely melted. (Be careful and do this in stages because chocolate burns.) Set aside to cool.

In another bowl, beat the eggs and the sugar with an electric mixer until light in color and thickened. Takes about 7-9 minutes. Add the cooled chocolate and combine.

Pour the batter into the prepared pan and bake for 1 1/2 hours.

Test the cake by inserting a toothpick in the center. If it comes out clean, it is done. If it is not done, place in oven for another five minutes and test again. Cool cake on rack for at half hour before unmolding.

Dust lightly with confection ers' sugar before serving.

Slice in small wedges and garnish with berries and ice cream.

Serves: 12.

Lemony Meringue Pie

Recipe Notes

This lemon filling is better than any that comes in a jar...called Lemon Curd. If you have to buy lemon curd, always add freshly grated lemon rind to make it taste better. You can use this lemon on cookies or blended with whipped cream and served with berries.

1	9" Prebaked pie shell
4	egg yolks
1 1/2	cups sugar
1/2	cup cornstarch
2	lemon rind, grated
1/3	cup lemon juice
2	cups water, boiling
1	tablespoon unsalted butter
1/8	teaspoon salt
4	egg whites, room temperature
1/4	teaspoon cream of tartar
2	tablespoons sugar

Instructions

Preheat oven to 400°.
Separate egg yolks and whites while eggs are cold. Let whites come to room temperature before beating.

Combine sugar, cornstarch and lemon rind; add boiling water. Cook until mixture is clear and thick, stirring constantly. Add egg yolks, lemon juice and butter. Beat well.

Cool 5 minutes.

Turn into baked pie shell and cover with meringue.

To make meringue:
Beat 4 egg whites until frothy. Add 2 Tablespoons of sugar slowly until stiff peaks form. Cover hot filling all the way to the edge, sealing the filling completely. Bake 8 minutes at 400 degrees. Let cool before slicing.

Option: Omit the meringue. Cool pie and top with whipped cream.

Serves: 6.

Lovely Lemon Mousse

Recipe Notes
Substitute lime for the lemon juice and zest and have another dessert.

Freezes well in dessert cups or small parfait glasses, but tastes best when defrosted. Decorate with whatever berries are in season and garnish with fresh mint.

A dessert that is made ahead and ready when you are.

4	cups heavy cream
1	cup condensed milk, sweetened
1	cup lemon juice, fresh
1	cup sugar
1	lemon zest, grated

Instructions

Combine cream, lime juice and condensed milk in a large mixing bowl and chill several hours. Refrigerate beaters, as well, the bowl.

Stir in sugar and whip until thick.

Turn into a serving dish or into individual dishes and refrigerate covered until firm; at least two hours. Sprinkle with grated lemon zest.

Serves: 8.

Mocha Mousse

<u>Recipe Notes</u>
I used to put this in a Mickey Mouse Mold and call it...yeah..you get it!..."Mocha Mouse'

6	egg yolks
3/4	cup sugar
1 1/2	cups strongly brewed coffee
2	envelopes Knox gelatin
1 1/2	pints heavy cream
1/2	cup Chocolate covered espresso beans

Instructions

In a 2 quart pot, on **low** heat, combine the egg yolks, sugar and coffee, stirring with a whisk until it forms a soft custard. It will not be thick enough to coat a spoon. Cook low and slow or it will be ugly.

Soften the gelatin in a 1/2 cup water. Stir into the custard and cool.

Whip the cream stiff and fold into the coffee mixture. Pour into a 2 quart mold and chill. Chill at least four hours.

Unmold and serve with Coffee Liqueur Sauce. Garnish with chocolate coffee beans.

See Coffee Liqueur Sauce Recipe.

Serves: 8.

Moscow Cream

Recipe Notes

This is a very elegant dessert that can be served on crystal plates or in martini glasses dressed with colorful fruit or sauces.

2	cups half and half
1/4	cup sugar
1	tablespoon Knox gelatin
1/4	cup water
2	cups sour cream
1	teaspoon vanilla

Instructions

Scald the half and half in a one quart pot but do no boil.

Soften the gelatin in the water and then dissolve in the scalded half and half. Cool to lukewarm.

Whisk in sour cream and vanilla. Chill in a fancy mold or in 8-10 small molds until firm, about four hours.

Unmold on dessert plate and surround with fresh fruit and a sprig of mint. Also could be served with Raspberry sauce.

Serves: 8.

Pashka

Recipe Notes
This dessert is so rich that it will serve an army in small pieces.

A bite of this with some fresh berries is very satisfying.

You could also take twelve small molds and make individual servings.

2	pounds cream cheese
1/4	cup egg beaters
2	sticks unsalted butter
2	teaspoons vanilla
1 1/2	cups Confectioners Sugar
3/4	cup toasted almonds, slivered

Instructions

In the large bowl of the mixer, combine the cream cheese, butter and egg yolks and let sit for at least two hours, to come to room temperature. Beat together at low speed until light and fluffy. then beat in sugar. Gently stir in the vanilla and almonds.

Wash and dry a two quart flower pot (6" wide at top) and line with a double thickness of cheesecloth that is long enough to extend up over the sides. Pour in the batter and then fold in the edges of the cheesecloth. Place pot in a bowl. Cover with plastic wrap and refrigerate overnight.

To unmold: pull up the cheesecloth to loosen the mold. Peel back the cheesecloth from the top to expose the pashka and then place a plate over the top an invert. Unwrap completely and garnish with fresh fruit or marron glaze*. Cut in small pieces from the top in wedges.

* Marron glaze are chestnuts cooked in syrup and cooked until candied. Very posh garnish! Available at fancy food stores.

Serves: 12.

Pat's Magic Bars

Recipe Notes
Pat Greenwald contributed these favorites from everyone's childhood.
The original recipe was on the can of sweetened condensed milk.
Pat has a whole repetoire of other great dishes that would fill a book of their own!
In truth, some of the best recipes, ever were on cans and boxes of products. You can
always start there in your search for a tried and true good result.

1	stick unsalted butter
1	cup Graham cracker crumbs, crumbled
6	ounces chocolate chips
1	cup coconut, flaked
1	cup nut pieces (variety of your choice)
15	ounces condensed milk, sweetened

Instructions

Preheat the oven to 350°.

Melt the butter in a 9 X 13 pan. Spread the Graham Cracker crumbs evenly over the butter.

Sprinkle with the chocolate chips and coconut, then scatter the chopped nuts over the top.

Drizzle the condensed milk over all.

Bake for 30-35 minutes. Cool completely before cutting into bars.

Makes 36.

Peach Kuchen

Recipe Notes

When peaches are ripe and beautiful or if you have really good canned peaches, this is easy and so good.

White nectarines are my favorite stone fruit. When they are ripe they are the most fragrant of all the summer fruit.

2	cups flour, sifted
1/4	teaspoon baking powder
1/2	teaspoon salt
1	cup sugar
6	peaches
1	teaspoon cinnamon
2	egg yolks
1	cup heavy cream
1/2	cup unsalted butter, room temperature

Instructions

Preheat oven to 400°.

Bring a pot of water to a boil. Slip the peaches in and blanch for about 50 seconds and then drop in ice water. Skin the peaches and set aside.

Sift flour, baking soda and salt with 2 tablespoons of sugar. Work in the butter with pastry blender until mixture looks like cornmeal. Pile into an 8" square cake pan and pat into an even layer over the bottom and halfway up on the sides. Cut the peaches in half and discard the pits. Lay over the pastry rounded side up. Sprinkle mixture of cinnamon and remaining sugar over the peaches and bake 15 minutes. Mix yolks and cream and pour over kuchen. Bake 30 minutes.

Test with a toothpick in the center, if it comes out clean, remove from oven. If toothpick is still wet, bake, testing at 5 minute intervals until done. Serve warm or at room temperature.

Serves: 8.

Index

the uncomplicated gourmet

Order Form

Fax Orders: 973-616-4422. Send this form.
Telephone Orders: 973-616-4411. Have your credit card ready.
Postal Orders: Elements for kitchen, bath, home, Inc,
            81 Hamburg Turnpike. Riverdale, NJ 07457

Name:
Address:
City:
State:
Zip:
Country:
Telephone:
Email:

Shipping via US Post office
Each Book costs $ 29.99 plus
U.S. Shipping charge $4.90 for first book and $ 3.20 for each additional book.

Payment:

___Check

___Credit Card ___Visa ___MasterCard

Card Number: _____

Name on Card: _____

Exp. Date: _____